The Necessity of Atheism

Also Available in the Freethought Library

*Debates between Believers and
Unbelievers*

*Joseph McCabe on the Christian
Myth*

The Necessity of Atheism
And Other Essays

Percy Bysshe Shelley

Prometheus Books
Buffalo, New York

Published 1993 by Prometheus Books

59 John Glenn Drive, Buffalo, New York 14228, 716-837-2475.
FAX: 716-835-6901.

Library of Congress Cataloging-in-Publication Data

Shelley, Percy Bysshe, 1792–1822.
    The necessity of atheism, and other essays / Percy Bysshe Shelley.
        p.   cm.
    Contents: Essay on Christianity — The necessity of atheism — On
life — On a future state — A refutation of deism.
    ISBN 0-87975-774-4
    1. Christianity—Controversial literature. 2. Religion—
Controversial literature. 3. Atheism. 4. Future life—
Controversial literature. 5. Deism—Controversial literature.
I. Title.
BL2745.S47   1993
210—dc20   92-40791
                                                                CIP

Printed in the United States of America on acid-free paper.

PERCY BYSSHE SHELLEY was born on August 4, 1792, at Field Place, near Horsham, Sussex, the son of Timothy (later Sir Timothy) Shelley. The young Shelley's independent nature became evident at Eton, where he rebelled against the school routine and even as a teenager earned the nicknames "the mad Shelley" and "Shelley the atheist."

In the autumn of 1810, Shelley entered Oxford University, where he made the acquaintance of Thomas Jefferson Hogg, who, like Shelley, was a skeptic and freethinker. With Hogg's support, Shelley published in 1811 his first pamphlet, "The Necessity of Atheism." After its authorship was revealed, Shelley, along with Hogg, was expelled from Oxford in March 1811. Making his way to London, Shelley met, and married, Harriet Westbrook, by whom he had a daughter, Ianthe Eliza, in 1813, and later a son, Charles Bysshe.

It was around 1814 that Shelley began to visit the household of William Godwin, the author of *Political Justice* and widower of Mary Wollstonecraft, who had written the progressive *A Vindication of the Rights of Women.*

Shelley was becoming increasingly estranged from his wife Harriet, whom he found incompatible. He discovered a far more suitable soulmate in the Godwins' daughter Mary, then seventeen. In 1816, Mary Godwin ran away to Switzerland with Shelley, now the heir to a comfortable estate. Despondent over losing her husband, Harriet committed suicide in 1817.

Despite (or, perhaps, partly because of) the turbulence of his private life, Shelley became a renowned literary figure, having published *Queen Mab* (1813); *Alastor, or the Spirit of Solitude; Mont Blanc* (both written in 1816); and *The Revolt of Islam* (1817). He was a friend of the poet Lord Byron and Leigh Hunt, the essayist and bold defender of the Romantics, including Shelley, Byron, and John Keats. Now married to Mary Godwin (who would win her own fame as the author of *Frankenstein*), Shelley moved permanently to Italy in 1818, and there wrote his greatest works, among them "Ode to the West Wind" (1819) and *Prometheus Unbound* (1820), which celebrated the freeing of the human mind from the trammels of outmoded religious belief.

Percy Bysshe Shelley's life was tragically cut short when he drowned in a boating accident off the northwest coast of Italy, near Viareggio, on July 8, 1822.

Contents

ESSAY ON CHRISTIANITY

A FRAGMENT

[NOTE.—The words between brackets are conjectures of Lady Shelley, by whom this fragment was first published.]

The Being who has influenced in the most memorable manner the opinions and the fortunes of the human species is Jesus Christ. At this day, his name is connected with the devotional feelings of two hundred millions of the race of man. The institutions of the most civilized portion of the globe derive their authority from the sanction of his doctrines; he is the hero, the God, of our popular religion. His extraordinary genius, the wide and rapid effect of his unexampled doctrines, his invincible gentleness and benignity, the devoted love borne to him by his adherents, suggested a persuasion to them that he was something divine. The supernatural events which the historians of this wonderful man subsequently asserted to have been connected with every gradation of his career, established the opinion.

* * * * * * *

The thoughts which the word "God" suggests to the human mind are susceptible of as many variations as human minds themselves. The Stoic, the Platonist, and the Epicurean, the Polytheist, the Dualist, and the Trinitarian, differ infinitely in their conceptions of its meanings. They agree only in considering it the most awful and most venerable of names, as a common term devised to express all of mystery, or majesty, or power, which the invisible world contains. And not only has every sect distinct conceptions of the application of this name, but scarcely two individuals of the same sect, who exercise in any degree the freedom of their judgment, or yield themselves with any candor of feeling to the influences of the visible world, find perfect coincidence of opinion to exist between them. It is [interesting] to inquire in what acceptation Jesus Christ employed this term.

We may conceive his mind to have been predisposed on this subject to adopt the opinions of his countrymen. Every human being is indebted for a multitude of his sentiments to the religion of his early years. Jesus Christ probably [studied] the historians of his country with the ardo1 of a spirit seeking after the truth. They were undoubtedly the companions of his childhood years, the food and nutriment and materials of his youthful meditations. The sublime dramatic poem entitled Job had familiarized his imagination with the boldest imagery afforded by the human mind and the material world. Ecclesiastes had diffused a seriousness and solemnity over the frame of his spirit, glowing with youthful hope, and [had] made audible to his listening heart—

> The still, sad music of humanity,
> Not harsh or grating, but of ample power
> To chasten and subdue.

He had contemplated his name as having been profanely perverted to the sanctioning of the most enormous and abominable crimes. We

can distinctly trace, in the tissue of his doctrines, the persuasion that God is some universal Being, differing from man and the mind
of man. According to Jesus Christ, God is
neither the Jupiter, who sends rain upon the
earth; nor the Venus, through whom all living
things are produced; nor the Vulcan, who pre-
sides over the terrestrial element of fire; nor
the Vesta, that preserves the light which is
enshrined in the sun and moon and stars. He
is neither the Proteus nor the Pan of the material world. But the word God, according to
the acceptation of Jesus Christ, unites all the
attributes which these denominations contain,
and is the [interpoint] and overruling Spirit
of all the energy and wisdom included within
the circle of existing things. It is important to
observe that the author of the Christian system
had a conception widely differing from the
gross imaginations of the vulgar relatively to
the ruling Power of the universe. He every-
where represents this Power as something
mysteriously and illimitably pervading the
frame of things.

*   *   *   *   *   *   *

"Blessed are the pure in heart, for they shall
see God." Blessed are those who have preserved internal sanctity of soul; who are conscious of no secret deceit; who are the same in
act as they are in desire; who conceal no
thought, no tendencies of thought, from their
own conscience; who are faithful and sincere
witnesses, before the tribunal of their own
judgments, of all that passes within their mind.
Such as these shall see God. What! after

death, shall their awakened eyes behold the King of Heaven? Shall they stand in awe before the golden throne on which he sits, and gaze upon the venerable countenance of the paternal Monarch? Is this the reward of the virtuous and the pure? These are the idle dreams of the visionary, or the pernicious representations of impostors, who have fabricated from the very materials of wisdom a cloak for their own dwarfish or imbecile conceptions.

Jesus Christ has said no more than the most excellent philosophers have felt and expressed —that virtue is its own reward. It is true that such an expression as he has used was prompted by the energy of genius, and was the overflowing enthusiasm of a poet; but it is not the less literally true [because] clearly repugnant to the mistaken conceptions of the multitude. God, it has been asserted, was contemplated by Jesus Christ as every poet and every philosopher must have contemplated that mysterious principle. He considered that venerable word to express the overruling Spirit of the collective energy of the moral and material world. He affirms, therefore, no more than that a simple, sincere mind is the indispensable requisite of true science and true happiness. He affirms that a being of pure and gentle habits will not fail, in every thought, in every object of every thought, to be aware of benignant visitings from the invisible energies by which he is surrounded.

Whosoever is free from the contamination of luxury and license, may go forth to the fields and to the woods, inhaling joyous renovation from the breath of Spring, or catching from the odors and sounds of Autumn some diviner mood of sweetest sadness, which improves the softened heart. Whosoever is no deceiver or destroyer of his fellow-men—no liar, no flatterer, no murderer—may walk among his species, deriving, from the communion with all which they contain of beautiful or of majestic, some intercourse with the Universal God. Whosoever has maintained with his own heart the strictest correspondence of confidence, who dares to examine and to estimate every imagination which suggests itself to his mind— whosoever is that which he designs to become, and only aspires to that which the divinity of his own nature shall consider and approve— he has already seen God.

We live and move and think; but we are not the creators of our own origin and existence. We are not the arbiters of every motion and of our own complicated nature; we are not the masters of our own imaginations and moods of mental being. There is a Power by which we are surrounded, like the atmosphere in which some motionless lyre is suspended, which visits with its breath our silent chords at will.

Our most imperial and stupendous qualities —those on which the majesty and the power of humanity is erected—are, relatively to the inferior portion of its mechanism, active and imperial; but they are the passive slaves of some higher and more omnipotent Power. This

Power is God; and those who have seen God have, in the period of their purer and more perfect nature, been harmonized by their own will to so exquisite [a] consentaneity of power as to give forth divinest melody, when the breath of universal being sweeps over their frame. That those who are pure in heart shall see God, and that virtue is its own reward, may be considered as equivalent assertions. The former of these propositions is a metaphorical repetition of the latter. The advocates of literal interpretation have been the most efficacious enemies of those doctrines whose nature they profess to venerate.

*   *   *   *   *   *   *

The doctrine of what some fanatics have termed "a peculiar Providence"—that is, of some power beyond and superior to that which ordinarily guides the operations of the Universe, interfering to punish the vicious and reward the virtuous—is explicitly denied by Jesus Christ. The absurd and execrable doctrine of vengeance, in all its shapes, seems to have been contemplated by this great moralist with the profoundest disapprobation; nor would he permit the most venerable of names to be perverted into a sanction for the meanest and most contemptible propensities incident to the nature of man. "Love your enemies, bless those who curse you, that ye may be the sons of your Heavenly Father, who makes the sun to shine on the good and on the evil, and the rain to fall on the just and unjust." How monstrous a calumny have not impostors dared to advance against the mild and gentle author of this just sentiment, and against the whole tenor of his doctrines and his life, overflowing with benevolence and forbearance and compassion! They have represented him asserting that the Omnipotent God—that merciful and benignant Power who scatters equally upon the beautiful earth all the elements of security and happiness—whose influences are distributed to all whose natures admit of a participation in them—who sends to the weak and vicious creatures of his will all the benefits which they are capable of sharing—that this God has devised a scheme whereby the body shall live after its apparent dissolution, and be rendered capable of indefinite torture. He is said to have compared the agonies which the vicious shall then endure to the excruciations of a living body bound among the flames, and being consumed sinew by sinew, and bone by bone.

And this is to be done, not because it is supposed (and the supposition would be sufficiently detestable) that the moral nature of the sufferer would be improved by his tortures —it is done because it *is just* to be done. My neighbor, or my servant, or my child, has done me an injury, and it is just that he should suffer an injury in return. Such is the doctrine which Jesus Christ summoned his whole resources of persuasion to oppose. "Love your enemies, bless those who curse you": such, he says, is the practice of God, and such must ye imitate if ye would be the children of God.

Jesus Christ would hardly have cited, as an example of all that is gentle and beneficent and compassionate, a Being who shall deliberately scheme to inflict on a large portion of the human race tortures indescribably intense and indefinitely protracted; who shall inflict them, too, without any mistake as to the true nature of pain—without any view to future good—merely because it is just.

This, and no other, is justice:—to consider, under all the circumstances and consequences of a particular case, how the greatest quantity and purest quality of happiness will ensue from any action; [this] is to be just, and there is no other justice. The distinction between justice and mercy was first imagined in the courts of tyrants. Mankind receive every relaxation of their tyranny as a circumstance of grace or favor. . . .

The nature of a narrow and malevolent spirit is so essentially incompatible with happiness as to render it inaccessible to the influences of the benignant God. All that his own perverse propensities will permit him to receive, that God abundantly pours forth upon him. If there is the slightest overbalance of happiness, which can be allotted to the most atrocious offender, consistently with the nature of things, that is rigidly made his portion by the ever-watchful Power of God. In every case, the human mind enjoys the utmost pleasure which it is capable of enjoying. God is represented by Jesus Christ as the Power from which, and through which, the streams of all that is excellent and delightful flow; the Power which models, as they pass, all the elements of this mixed universe to the purest and most perfect shape which it belongs to their nature to assume. Jesus Christ attributes to this Power the faculty of Will. How far such a doctrine, in its ordinary sense, may be philosophically true, or how far Jesus Christ intentionally availed himself of a metaphor easily understood, is foreign to the subject to consider. This much is certain, that Jesus Christ represents God as the fountain of all goodness, the eternal enemy of pain and evil, the uniform and unchanging motive of the salutary operations of the material world. The supposition that this cause is excited to action by some principle analogous to the human will, adds weight to the persuasion that it is foreign to its beneficent nature to inflict the slightest pain. According to Jesus Christ, and according to the indisputable facts of the case, some evil spirit has dominion in this imperfect world. But there will come a time when the human mind shall be visited exclusively by the influences of the benignant Power. Men shall die, and their bodies shall rot under the ground; all the organs through which their knowledge and their feelings have flowed, or in which they have originated, shall assume other forms, and become ministrant to purposes the most foreign from their former tendencies. There is a time when we shall neither be heard nor be seen by the multitude of beings like ourselves by whom we have been so long surrounded. They shall go to graves; where then?

It appears that we moulder to a heap of senseless dust; to a few worms, that arise and perish, like ourselves. Jesus Christ asserts that these appearances are fallacious, and that a gloomy and cold imagination alone suggests the conception that thought can cease to be. Another and a more extensive state of being, rather than the complete extinction of being, will follow from that mysterious change which we call Death. There shall be no misery, no pain, no fear. The empire of evil spirits extends not beyond the boundaries of the grave. The unobscured irradiations from the fountain-fire of all goodness shall reveal all that is mysterious and unintelligible, until the mutual communications of knowledge and of happiness throughout all thinking natures constitute a harmony of good that ever varies and never ends.

This is Heaven, when pain and evil cease, and when the the Benignant Principle, untrammeled and uncontrolled, visits in the fullness of its power the universal frame ôf things. Human life, with all its unreal ills and transitory hopes, is as a dream, which departs before the dawn, leaving no trace of its evanescent hues. All that it contains of pure or of divine visits the passive mind in some serenest mood. Most holy are the feelings through which our fellow beings are rendered dear and [venerable] to the heart. The remembrance of their sweetness, and the completion of the hopes which they [excite], constitute. when we awaken from the sleep of life, the fulfillment of the prophecies of its most majestic and beautiful visions.

We die, says Jesus Christ; and, when we awaken from the languor of disease, the glories and the happiness of Paradise are around us. All evil and pain have ceased forever. Our happiness also corresponds with, and is adapted to, the nature of what is most excellent in our being. We see God, and we see that he is good. How delightful a picture, even if it be not true! How magnificent is the conception which this bold theory suggests to the contemplation, even if it be no more than the imagination of some sublimest and most holy poet, who, impressed with the loveliness and majesty of his own nature, is impatient and discontented with the narrow limits which this imperfect life and the dark grave have assigned the conception of this daring mind. It is not to be believed that Hell, or punishment, was the conception of this daring mind. It is not to be believed that the most prominent group of this picture, which is framed so heart-moving and lovely—the accomplishment of all human hope, the extinction of all morbid fear and anguish—would consists of millions of sensitive beings enduring, in every variety of torture which Omniscient vengeance could invent, immortal agony.

Jesus Christ opposed with earnest eloquence the panic fears and hateful superstitions which have enslaved mankind for ages. Nations had risen against nations, employing the subtlest devices of mechanism and mind to waste, and excruciate, and overthrow. The great community of mankind had been subdivided into ten thousand communities, each organized for the ruin of the other. Wheel within wheel, the vast machine was instinct with the restless spirit of desolation. Pain had been inflicted; therefore, pain should be inflicted in return. Retaliation of injuries is the only remedy which can be applied to violence, because it teaches the injurer the true nature of his own conduct, and operates as a warning against its repetition. Nor must the same measure of calamity be returned as was received. If a man borrows a certain sum from me, he is bound to repay that sum. Shall no more be required of the enemy who destroys my reputation, or ravages my fields? It is just that he should suffer ten times the loss which he has inflicted, that the legitimate consequences of his deed may never be obliterated from his remembrance, and that others may clearly discern and feel the danger of invading the peace of human society. Such reasonings, and the impetuous feelings arising from them, have armed nation against nation, family against family, man against man. . . .

The emptiness and folly of retaliation are apparent from every example which can be brought forward. Not only Jesus Christ, but the most eminent professors of every sect of philosophy, have reasoned against this futile superstition. Legislation is, in one point of view, to be considered as an attempt to provide against the excesses of this deplorable mistake. It professes to assign the penalty of all private injuries, and denies to individuals the right of vindicating their proper cause. This end is certainly not attained without some accommodation to the propensities which it desires to destroy. Still, it recognizes no principle but the production of the greatest eventual good with the least immediate injury; and regards the torture, or the death, of any human being as unjust, of whatever mischief he may have been the author, so that the result shall not more than compensate for the immediate pain.

Mankind, transmitting from generation to generation the legacy of accumulated vengeances, and pursuing with the feelings of duty the misery of their fellow-beings, have not failed to attribute to the Universal Cause a character analogous with their own. The image of this invisible, mysterious Being is more or less excellent and perfect—resembles more or less its original—in proportion to the perfection of the mind on which it is impressed. Thus, that nation which has arrived at the highest step in the scale of moral progression will believe most purely in that God, the knowledge of whose real attributes is considered as the firmest basis of the true religion. The reason of the belief of each individual, also, will be so far regulated by his conceptions of what is good. Thus, the conceptions which any nation or individual entertains of the God of its popular worship may be inferred from their own actions and opinions, which are the subjects of their approbation among their fellowmen. Jesus Christ instructed his disciples to be perfect, as their Father in Heaven is perfect, declaring at the same time his belief that human perfection requires the refraining from revenge and retribution in any of its various shapes.

The perfection of the human and the divine

character is thus asserted to be the same. Man, by resembling God, fulfils most accurately the tendencies of his nature; and God comprehends within himself all that constitutes human perfection. Thus, God is a model through which the excellence of man is to be estimated, whilst the *abstract* perfection of the human character is the type of the *actual* perfection of the divine. It is not to be believed that a person of such comprehensive views as Jesus Christ could have fallen into so manifest a contradiction as to assert that men would be tortured after death by that Being whose character is held up as a model to human kind, because he is incapable of malevolence and revenge. All the arguments which have been brought forward to justify retribution fail, when retribution is destined neither to operate as an example to other agents, nor to the offender himself. How feeble such reasoning is to be considered, has been already shown; but it is the character of an evil Daemon to consign the beings whom he has endowed with sensation to unprofitable anguish. The peculiar circumstances attendant on the conception of God casting sinners to burn in Hell forever, combine to render that conception the most perfect specimen of the greatest imaginable crime. Jesus Christ represented God as the principle of all good, the source of all happiness, the wise and benevolent Creator and Preserver of all living things. But the interpreters of his doctrines have confounded the good and the evil principle. They observed the emanations of their universal natures to be inextricably entangled in the world, and, trembling before the power of the cause of all things, addressed to it such flattery as is acceptable to the ministers of human tyranny, attributing love and wisdom to those energies which they felt to be exerted indifferently for the purposes of benefit and calamity.

Jesus Christ expressly asserts that distinction between the good and evil principle which it has been the practice of all theologians to confound. How far his doctrines, or their interpretation, may be true, it would scarcely have been worthwhile to inquire, if the one did not afford an example and an incentive to the attainment of true virtue, whilst the other holds out a sanction and apology for every species of mean and cruel vice.

It cannot be precisely ascertained in what degree Jesus Christ accommodated his doctrines to the opinions of his auditors; or in what degree he really said all that he is related to have said. He has left no written record of himself, and we are compelled to judge from the imperfect and obscure information which his biographers (persons certainly of very undisciplined and undiscriminating minds) have transmitted to posterity. These writers (our only guides) impute sentiments to Jesus Christ which flatly contradict each other. They represent him as narrow, superstitious, and exquisitely vindictive and malicious. They insert, in the midst of a strain of impassioned eloquence or sagest exhortation, a sentiment only remarkable for its naked and driveling folly. But it is not difficult to distinguish the inventions by which these historians have filled up the interstices of tradition, or corrupted the simplicity of truth, from the real character of their rude amazement. They have left sufficiently clear indications of the genuine character of Jesus Christ to rescue it forever from the imputations cast upon it by their ignorance and fanaticism. We discover that he is the enemy of oppression and of falsehood; that he is the advocate of equal justice; that he is neither disposed to sanction bloodshed nor deceit, under whatsoever pretenses their practice may be vindicated. We discover that he was a man of meek and majestic demeanor, calm in danger; of natural and simple thought and habits; beloved to adoration by his adherents; unmoved, solemn, and severe.

It is utterly incredible that this man said that if you hate your enemy you would find it to your account to return him good for evil, since, by such a temporary oblivion of vengeance, you would heap coals of fire on his head. Where such contradictions occur, a favorable construction is warranted by the general innocence of manners and comprehensiveness of views which he is represented to possess. The rule of criticism to be adopted in judging of the life, actions, and words of a man who has acted any conspicuous part in the revolutions of the world, should not be narrow. We ought to form a general image of his character and of his doctrines, and refer to this whole the distinct portions of actions and speech by which they are diversified. It is not here asserted that no contradictions are to be admitted to have taken place in the system of Jesus

Christ, between doctrines promulgated in different states of feeling or information, or even such as are implied in the enunciation of a scheme of thought, various and obscure through its immensity and depth. It is not asserted that no degree of human indignation ever hurried him, beyond the limits which his calmer mood had placed, to disapprobation against vice and folly. Those deviations from the history of his life are alone to be vindicated which represent his own essential character in contradiction with itself.

Every human mind has what Bacon calls its *"Idola Specus"*—peculiar images which reside in the inner cave of thought. These constitute the essential and distinctive character of every human being; to which every action and every word have intimate relation; and by which, in depicting a character, the genuineness and meaning of these words and actions are to be determined. Every fanatic or enemy of virtue is not at liberty to misrepresent the greatest geniuses and most heroic defenders of all that is valuable in this mortal world. History, to gain any credit, must contain some truth, and that truth shall thus be made a sufficient indication of prejudice and deceit.

With respect to the miracles which these biographers have related, I have already declined to enter into any discussion on their nature or their existence. The supposition of their falsehood or their truth would modify in no degree the hues of the picture which is attempted to be delineated. . . . Much, however, of what his (Christ's) biographers have asserted is not to be rejected merely because in-

ferences inconsistent with the general spirit of
his system are to be adduced from its admission. Jesus Christ did what every other reformer who has produced any considerable effect upon the world has done. He accommodated his doctrines to the prepossessions of
those whom he addressed. He used a language for this view sufficiently familiar to
our comprehensions. He said,—However new
or strange my doctrines may appear to you,
they are in fact only the restoration and
re-establishment of those original institutions and ancient customs of your own
law and religion. The constitution of your
faith and policy, although perfect in their
origin, have become corrupt and altered, and
have fallen into decay. I profess to restore
them to their pristine authority and splendor.
"Think not that I am come to destroy the Law
and the Prophets. I am come not to destroy,
but to fulfil. Till heaven and earth pass away,
one jot or one tittle shall in nowise pass away
from the Law, till all be fulfilled." Thus, like
a skilful orator (see Cicero, *De Oratore*), he
secures the prejudices of his auditors, and in-
duces them, by his professions of sympathy
with their feelings, to enter with a willing
mind into the exposition of his own. The art
of persuasion differs from that of reasoning;
and it is of no small moment, to the success
even of a true cause, that the judges who are
to determine on its merits should be free from
those national and religious predilections
which render the multitude both deaf and
blind,

Let not this practice be considered as an
unworthy artifice. It were best for the cause
of reason that mankind should acknowledge
no authority but its own; but it is useful, to a
certain extent, that they should not consider
those institutions which they have been habitu-
ated to reverence as opposing an obstacle to
its admission. All reformers have been compelled to practice this misrepresentation of
their own true feelings and opinions. It is
deeply to be lamented that a word should ever
issue from human lips which contains the
minutest alloy of dissimulation, or simulation,
or hypocrisy, or exaggeration, or anything but
the precise and rigid image which is present
to the mind, and which ought to dictate the
expression. But the practice of utter sincerity
towards other men would avail to no good end,
if they were incapable of practising it towards
their own minds. In fact, truth cannot be
communicated until it is perceived. The interests, therefore, of truth require that an orator should, as far as possible, produce in his
hearers that state of mind on which alone his
exhortations could fairly be contemplated and
examined.

Having produced this favorable disposition
of mind, Jesus Christ proceeds to qualify, and
finally to abrogate, the system of the Jewish
law. He descants upon its insufficiency as a
code of moral conduct, which it professed to
be, and absolutely selects the law of retaliation as an instance of the absurdity and immorality of its institutions. The conclusion
of the speech is in a strain of the most daring

and most impassioned speculation. He seems emboldened by the success of his exculpation to the multitude, to declare in public the utmost singularity of his faith. He tramples upon all received opinions, on all the cherished luxuries and superstitions of mankind. He bids them cast aside the claims of custom and blind faith by which they have been encompassed from the very cradle of their being, and receive the imitator and minister of the Universal God.

*   *   *   *   *   *   *   *

With all those who are truly wise, there will be an entire community, not only of thoughts and feelings, but also of external possessions. Insomuch, therefore, as ye live [wisely], ye may enjoy the community of whatsoever benefits arise from the inventions of civilized life. They are of value only for purposes of mental power; they are of value only as they are capable of being shared and applied to the common advantage of philosophy; and, if there be no love among men, whatever institutions they may frame must be subservient to the same purpose —to the continuance of inequality. If there be no love among men, it is best that he who sees through the hollowness of their professions should fly from their society, and suffice to his own soul. In wisdom, he will thus lose nothing; in power, he will gain everything. In proportion to the love existing among men, so will be the community of property and power. Among true and real friends, all is common; and, were ignorance and envy and superstition banished from the world, all mankind would be friends. The only perfect and genuine republic is that which comprehends every living being. Those distinctions which have been artificially set up, of nations, societies, families, and religions, are only general names, expressing the abhorrence and contempt with which men blindly consider their fellow-men. I love my country; I love the city in which I was born, my parents, my wife, and the children of my care; and to this city, this woman, and this nation, it is incumbent on me to do all the benefit in my power. To what do these distinctions point, but to an evident denial of the duty which humanity imposes on you, of doing every possible good to every individual, under whatever denomination he may be comprehended, to whom you have the power of doing it? You ought to love all mankind; nay, every individual of mankind. You ought not to love the individuals of your domestic circle less, but to love those who exist beyond it more. Once make the feelings of confidence and of affection universal, and the distinctions of property and power will vanish; nor are they to be abolished without substituting something equivalent in mischief to them, until all mankind shall acknowledge an entire community of rights.

But, as the shades of night are dispelled by the faintest glimmerings of dawn, so shall the minutest progress of the benevolent feelings disperse, in some degree, the gloom of tyranny, and [curb the] ministers of mutual suspicion and abhorrence. Your physical wants are few, whilst those of your mind and heart cannot be numbered or described, from their multitude and complication. To secure the gratification of the former, you have made yourselves the bond-slaves of each other.

They have cultivated these meaner wants to so great an excess as to judge nothing so valuable or desirable [as] what relates to their gratification. Hence has arisen a system of passions which loses sight of the end they were originally awakened to attain. Fame, power, and gold, are loved for their own sakes—are worshipped with a blind, habitual idolatry. The pageantry of empire, and the fame of irresistible might, are contemplated by the possessor with unmeaning complacency, without a retrospect to the properties which first made him consider them of value. It is from the cultivation of the most contemptible properties of human nature that discord and torpor and indifference, by which the moral universe is disordered, essentially depend. So long as these are the ties by which human society is connected, let it not be admitted that they are fragile.

Before man can be free, and equal, and truly wise, he must cast aside the chains of habit and superstition; he must strip sensuality of its pomp, and selfishness of its excuses, and contemplate actions and objects as they really are. He will discover the wisdom of universal love; he will feel the meanness and the injustice of sacrificing the reason and the liberty of his fellowmen to the indulgence of his physical appetites, and becoming a party to their degradation by the consummation of his own.

Such, with those differences only incidental

to the age and state of society in which they were promulgated, appear to have been the doctrines of Jesus Christ. It is not too much to assert that they have been the doctrines of every just and compassionate mind that ever speculated on the social nature of man. The dogma of the equality of mankind has been advocated, with various success, in different ages of the world. It was imperfectly understood, but a kind of instinct in its favor influenced considerably the practice of ancient Greece and Rome. Attempts to establish usages founded on this dogma have been made in modern Europe, in several instances, since the revival of literature and the arts. Rousseau has vindicated this opinion with all the eloquence of sincere and earnest faith; and is, perhaps, the philosopher among the moderns who, in the structure of his feelings and understanding, resembles most nearly the mysterious sage of Judea. It is impossible to read those passionate words in which Jesus Christ upbraids the pusillanimity and sensuality of mankind, without being strongly reminded of the more connected and systematic enthusiasm of Rousseau. "No man," says Jesus Christ, "can serve two masters. Take, therefore, no thought for tomorrow, for the morrow shall take thought for the things of itself. Sufficient unto the day is the evil thereof." If we would profit by the wisdom of a sublime and poetical mind, we must beware of the vulgar error of interpreting literally every expression it employs. Nothing can well be more remote from truth than the literal and strict construction of such expressions as Jesus Christ delivers, or than [to imagine that] it were best for man that he should abandon all his acquirements in physical and intellectual science, and depend on the spontaneous productions of nature for his subsistence. Nothing is more obviously false than that the remedy for the inequality among men consists in their return to the condition of savages and beasts. Philosophy will never be understood if we approach the study of its mysteries with so narrow and illiberal conceptions of its universality. Rousseau certainly did not mean to persuade the immense population of his country to abandon all the arts of life, destroy their habitations and their temples, and become the inhabitants of the woods. He addressed the most enlightened of his compatriots, and endeavored to persuade them to set the example of a pure and simple life, by placing in the strongest point of view his conceptions of the calamitous and diseased aspect which, overgrown as it is with the vices of sensuality and selfishness, is exhibited by civilized society. Nor can it be believed that Jesus Christ endeavored to prevail on the inhabitants of Jerusalem neither to till their fields, nor to frame a shelter against the sky, nor to provide food for the morrow. He simply exposes, with the passionate rhetoric of enthusiastic love towards all human beings, the miseries and mischiefs of that system which makes all things subservient to the subsistence of the material frame of man. He warns them that no man can serve two masters—God and Mammon; that it is impossible at once to be high-minded and just and wise, and to comply with the accustomed forms of human society, seek power, wealth, or empire, either from the idolatry of habit, or as the direct instruments of sensual gratification. He instructs them that clothing and food and shelter are not, as they suppose, the true end of human life, but only certain means, to be valued in proportion to their subserviency to that end. This means it is the right of every human being to possess, and that in the same degree. In this respect, the fowls of the air and the lilies of the field are examples for the imitation of mankind. They are clothed and fed by the Universal God. Permit, therefore, the Spirit of this benignant Principle to visit your intellectual frame, or, in other words, become just and pure. When you understand the degree of attention which the requisitions of your physical nature demand, you will perceive how little labor suffices for their satisfaction. Your Heavenly Father knoweth you have need of these things. The universal Harmony, or Reason, which makes your passive frame of thought its dwelling, in proportion to the purity and majesty of its nature will instruct you, if ye are willing to attain that exalted condition, in what manner to possess all the objects necessary for your material subsistence. All men are [impelled] to become thus pure and happy. All men are called to participate in the community of Nature's gifts. The man who has fewest bodily wants approaches nearest to the Divine Nature. Satisfy these wants at the cheapest rate, and expend the remaining energies of your nature

in the attainment of virtue and knowledge.
The mighty frame of the wonderful and lovely
world is the food of your contemplation, and
living beings who resemble your own nature,
and are bound to you by similarity of sensations, are destined to be the nutriment of your
affection; united, they are the consummation
of the widest hopes your mind can contain.
Ye can expend thus no labor on mechanism
consecrated to luxury and pride. How abund-
ant will not be your progress in all that truly
ennobles and extends human nature! By
rendering yourselves thus worthy, ye will be as
free in your imaginations as the swift and
many-colored fowls of the air, and as beautiful
in pure simplicity as the lilies of the field. In
proportion as mankind becomes wise—yes, in
exact proportion to that wisdom—should be the
extinction of the unequal system under which
they now subsist. Government is, in fact, the
mere badge of their depravity. They are so
little aware of the inestimable benefits of
mutual love as to indulge, without thought, and
almost without motive, in the worst excesses
of selfishness and malice. Hence, without
graduating human society into a scale of empire and subjection, its very existence has become impossible. It is necessary that universal
benevolence should supersede the regulations
of precedent and prescription, before these
regulations can safely be abolished. Meanwhile, their very subsistence depends on the
system of injustice and violence which they
have been devised to palliate. They suppose
men endowed with the power of deliberating

and determining for their equals; whilst these men, as frail and as ignorant as the multitude whom they rule, possess, as a practical consequence of this power, the right which they of necessity exercise to prevent (together with their own) the physical and moral and intellectual nature of all mankind.

It is the object of wisdom to equalize the distinctions on which this power depends, by exhibiting in their proper worthlessness the objects, a contention concerning which renders its existence a necessary evil. The evil, in fact, is virtually abolished wherever *justice* is practised; and it is abolished in precise proportion to the prevalence of true virtue. . . .

To the accomplishment of such mighty hopes were the views of Jesus Christ extended; such did he believe to be the tendency of his doctrines—the abolition of artificial distinctions among mankind, so far as the love which it becomes all human beings to bear towards each other, and the knowledge of truth from which that love will never fail to be produced, avail to their destruction. A young man came to Jesus Christ, struck by the miraculous dignity and simplicity of his character, and attracted by the words of power which he uttered. He demanded to be considered as one of the followers of his creed. "Sell all that thou hast," replied the philosopher; "give it to the poor, and follow me." But the young man had large possessions, and he went away sorrowing.

The system of equality was attempted, after Jesus Christ's death, to be carried into effect by his followers. "They that believed had all things in common; they sold their possessions and goods, and parted them to all men, as every man had need; and they continued daily with one accord in the temple, and, breaking bread from house to house, did eat their meat with gladness and singleness of heart." (Acts ii).

The practical application of the doctrines of strict justice to a state of society established in its contempt, was such as might have been expected. After the transitory glow of enthusiasm had faded from the minds of men, precedent and habit resumed their empire; they broke like an universal deluge on one shrinking and solitary island. Men to whom birth had allotted ample possession looked with complacency on sumptuous apartments and luxurious food, and those ceremonials of delusive majesty which surround the throne of power and the court of wealth. Men, from whom these things were withheld by their condition, began again to gaze with stupid envy on pernicious splendor; and, by desiring the false greatness of another's state, to sacrifice the intrinsic dignity of their own. The demagogues of the infant republic of the Christian sect, attaining, through eloquence or artifice, to influence amongst its members, first violated (under the pretense of watching over their integrity) the institutions established for the common and equal benefit of all. These demagogues artfully silenced the voice of the moral sense among them by engaging them to attend, not so much to the cultivation of a virtuous and happy life in this moral sense, as to the attainment of a fortunate condition after death; not so much to the consideration of those means by which the state of man is adorned and improved, as an inquiry into the secrets of the connection between God and the world—things which, they well knew, were not to be explained, or even to be conceived. The system of equality which they established necessarily fell to the ground, because it is a system that must result from, rather than precede, the moral improvement of human kind. It was a circumstance of no moment that the first adherents of the system of Jesus Christ cast their property into a common stock. The same degree of real community of property could have subsisted without this formality, which served only to extend a temptation of dishonesty to the treasurers of so considerable a patrimony. Every man, in proportion to his virtue, considers himself, with respect to the great community of mankind, as the steward and guardian of their interests in the property which he chances to possess. Every man, in proportion to his wisdom, sees the manner in which it is his duty to employ the resources which the consent of mankind has intrusted to his discretion. Such is the [annihilation] of the unjust inequality of powers and conditions existing in the world; and so gradually and inevitably is the progress of equality accommodated to the progress of wisdom and of virtue among mankind.

Meanwhile, some benefit has not failed to flow from the imperfect attempts which have been made to erect a system of equal rights to property and power upon the basis of arbitrary institutions. They have undoubtedly, in every case, from the instability of their formation, failed Still, they constitute a record of those epochs at which a true sense of justice suggested itself to the understandings of men, so that they consented to forego all the cherished delights of luxury, all the habitual gratifications arising out of the possessions or the expectation of power, all the superstitions with which the accumulated authority of ages had made them dear and venerable. They are so many trophies erected in the enemy's land, to mark the limits of the victorious progress of truth and justice.

Jesus Christ did not fail to advert to the——

[THE REST IS WANTING]

THE NECESSITY OF ATHEISM

[NOTE.—*The Necessity of Atheism* was published by Shelley in 1811. In 1813 he printed a revised and expanded version of it as one of the notes to his poem *Queen Mab*. The revised and expanded version is the one here reprinted.]

THERE IS NO GOD

This negation must be understood solely to affect a creative Deity. The hypothesis of a pervading Spirit coeternal with the universe remains unshaken.

A close examination of the validity of the proofs adduced to support any proposition is the only secure way of attaining truth, on the advantages of which it is unnecessary to descant: our knowledge of the existence of a Deity is a subject of such importance that it cannot be too minutely investigated; in consequence of this conviction we proceed briefly and impartially to examine the proofs which have been adduced. It is necessary first to consider the nature of belief.

When a proposition is offered to the mind, it perceives the agreement or disagreement of the ideas of which it is composed. A perception of their agreement is termed *belief*. Many obstacles frequently prevent this perception from being immediate; these the mind attempts to remove in order that the perception may be distinct. The mind is active in the investigation in order to perfect the state of perception of the relation which the component ideas of the proposition bear to each, which is passive: the investigation being confused with the per-

ception has induced many falsely to imagine
that the mind is active in belief,—that belief
is an act of volition,—in consequence of which
it may be regulated by the mind. Pursuing, con-
tinuing this mistake, they have attached a degree of criminality to disbelief; of which, in its
nature, it is incapable: it is equally incapable
of merit.

Belief, then, is a passion, the strength of
which, like every other passion, is in precise
proportion to the degrees of excitement.

The degrees of excitement are three.

The senses are the sources of all knowledge
to the mind; consequently their evidence claims
the strongest assent.

The decision of the mind, founded upon our
own experience, derived from these sources,
claims the next degree.

The experience of others, which addresses
itself to the former one, occupies the lowest
degree.

(A graduated scale, on which should be
marked the capabilities of propositions to approach to the test of the senses, would be a
just barometer of the belief which ought to be
attached to them.)

Consequently no testimony can be admitted
which is contrary to reason; reason is founded
on the evidence of our senses.

Every proof may be referred to one of these
three divisions: it is to be considered what
arguments we receive from each of them, which
should convince us of the existence of a Deity.

1st, The evidence of the senses. If the Deity
should appear to us, if he should convince our

senses of his existence, this revelation would necessarily command belief. Those to whom the Deity has thus appeared have the strongest possible conviction of his existence. But the God of Theologians is incapable of local visibility.

2d, Reason. It is urged that man knows that whatever is must either have had a beginning, or have existed from all eternity: he also knows that whatever is not eternal must have had a cause. When this reasoning is applied to the universe, it is necessary to prove that it was created: until that is clearly demonstrated we may reasonably suppose that it has endured from all eternity. We must prove design before we can infer a designer. The only idea which we can form of causation is derivable from the constant conjunction of objects, and the consequent inference of one from the other. In a case where two propositons are diametrically opposite, the mind believes that which is least incomprehensible;—it is easier to suppose that the universe has existed from all eternity than to conceive a being beyond its limits capable of creating it: if the mind sinks beneath the weight of one, is it an alleviation to increase the intolerability of the burthen?

The other argument, which is founded on a man's knowledge of his own existence, stands thus. A man knows not only that he now is, but that once he was not; consequently there must have been a cause. But our idea of causation is alone derivable from the constant conjunction of objects and the consequent inference of one from the other; and, reasoning experimentally, we can only infer from effects causes exactly adequate to those effects. But there certainly is a generative power which is effected by certain instruments: we cannot prove that it is inherent in these instruments; nor is the contrary hypothesis capable of demonstration: we admit that the generative power is incomprehensible; but to suppose that the same effect is produced by an eternal, omniscient, omnipotent being leaves the cause in the same obscurity, but renders it more incomprehensible.

3d, Testimony. It is required that testimony should not be contrary to reason. The testimony that the Deity convinces the senses of men of his existence can only be admitted by us, if our mind considers it less probable that these men should have been deceived than that the Deity should have appeared to them. Our reason can never admit the testimony of men, who not only declare that they were eye-witnesses of miracles, but that the Deity was irrational; for he commanded that he should be believed, he proposed the highest rewards for faith, eternal punishments for disbelief. We can only command voluntary actions; belief is not an act of volition; the mind is even passive, or involuntarily active; from this it is evident that we have no sufficient testimony, or rather that testimony is insufficient to prove the being of a God. It has been before shown that it cannot be deduced from reason. They alone, then, who have been convinced by the evidence of the senses can believe it.

Hence it is evident that, having no proofs from either of the three sources of conviction,

the mind *cannot* believe the existence of a creative God: it is also evident that, as belief is a
passion of the mind, no degree of criminality
is attachable to disbelief; and that they only
are reprehensible who neglect to remove the
false medium through which their mind views
any subject of discussion. Every reflecting
mind must acknowledge that there is no proof
of the existence of a Deity.

God is an hypothesis, and, as such, stands in
need of proof: the *onus probandi* rests on the
theist. Sir Isaac Newton says: *Hypotheses non
fingo, quicquid enim ex phaenomenis non deduc-
itur hypothesis, vocanda est, et hypothesis vel
metaphysicae, vel physicae, vel qualitatum oc-
cultarum, seu mechanicae, in philosophia locum
non habent.* To all proofs of the existence of a
creative God apply this valuable rule. We see a
variety of bodies possessing a variety of powers: we merely know their effects; we are in a
state of ignorance with respect to their essences
and causes. These Newton calls the phenomena
of things; but the pride of philosophy is unwill-
ing to admit its ignorance of their causes. From
the phenomena, which are the objects of our
senses, we attempt to infer a cause, which we
call God, and gratuitously endow it with all
negative and contradictory qualities. From this
hypothesis we invent this general name, to conceal our ignorance of causes and essences. The
being called God by no means answers with the
conditions prescribed by Newton; it bears
every mark of a veil woven by philosophical
conceit, to hide the ignorance of philosophers
even from themselves. They borrow the threads

of its texture from the anthropomorphism of the vulgar. Words have been used by sophists for the same purposes, from the occult qualities of the peripatetics to the *effluvium* of Boyle and the *crinities* or *nebulae* of Herschel. God is represented as infinite, eternal, incomprehensible; he is contained under every predicate in non that the logic of ignorance could fabricate. Even his worshippers allow that it is impossible to form any idea of him: they exclaim with the French poet,

Pour dire ce qu'il est, il faut être lui-même.

Lord Bacon says that atheism leaves to man reason, philosophy, natural piety, laws, reputation, and everything that can serve to conduct him to virtue; but superstition destroys all these, and erects itself into a tyranny over the understandings of men: hence atheism never disturbs the government, but renders man more clear-sighted, since he sees nothing beyond the boundaries of the present life.—Bacon's *Moral Essays.*

The* first theology of man made him first fear and adore the elements themselves, the gross and material objects of nature; he next paid homage to the agents controlling the elements, lower genies, heroes or men gifted with great qualities. By force of reflection he sought to simplify things by submitting all nature to a single agent, spirit, or universal soul, which gave movement to nature and all its branches.

---

*Beginning here, and to the paragraph ending with "Système de la Nature," Shelley wrote in French. A free translation has been substituted.

Mounting from cause to cause, mortal man has ended by seeing nothing; and it is in this obscurity that he has placed his God; it is in this darksome abyss that his uneasy imagination has always labored to fabricate chimeras, which will continue to afflict him until his knowledge of nature chases these phantoms which he has always so adored.

If we wish to explain our ideas of the Divinity, we shall be obliged to admit that, by the word *God*, man has never been able to designate but the most hidden, the most distant and the most unknown cause of the effects which he saw; he has made use of his word only when the play of natural and known causes ceased to be visible to him; as soon as he lost the thread of these causes, or when his mind could no longer follow the chain, he cut the difficulty and ended his researches by calling God the last of the causes, that is to say, that which is beyond all causes that he knew; thus he but assigned a vague denomination to an unknown cause, at which his laziness or the limits of his knowledge forced him to stop. Every time we say that God is the author of some phenomenon, that signifies that we are ignorant of how such a phenomenon was able to operate by the aid of forces or causes that we know in nature. It is thus that the generality of mankind, whose lot is ignorance, attributes to the Divinity, not only the unusual effects which strike them, but moreover the most simple events, of which the causes are the most simple to understand by whomsoever is able to study them. In a word, man has always respected unknown causes, surprising effects that his ignorance kept him from unraveling. It was on this debris of nature that man raised the imaginary colossus of the Divinity.

If ignorance of nature gave birth to gods, knowledge of nature is made for their destruction. In proportiton as man taught himself, his strength and his resources augmented with his knowledge; science, the arts, industry, furnished him assistance; experience reassured him or procured for him means of resistance to the efforts of many causes which ceased to alarm as soon as they became understood. In a word, his terrors dissipated in the same proportion as his mind became enlightened. The educated man ceases to be superstitious.

It is only by hearsay (by word of mouth passed down from generation to generation) that whole peoples adore the God of their fa thers and of their priests: authority, confidence, submission and custom with them take the place of conviction or of proofs: they prostrate themselves and pray, because their fathers taught them to prostrate themselves and pray: but why did their fathers fall on their knees? That is because, in primitive times, their legislators and their guides made it their duty. "Adore and believe," they said, "the gods whom you cannot understand; have confidence in our profound wisdom; we know more than you about Divinity." But why should I come to you? It is because God willed it thus; it is because God will punish you if you dare resist. But this God, is not he, then, the thing in question? However, man has always traveled in this vicious circle; his slothful mind has always made him find it easier to accept the judgment of others. All religious notions are founded solely on authority; all the religions of the world forbid examination and do not want one to reason; authority wants one to believe in God; this God is himself founded only on the authority of a few men who pretend to know him, and to come in his name and announce him on earth. A God made by man undoubtedly has need of man to make himself known to man.

Should it not, then, be for the priests, the inspired, the metaphysicians that should be reserved the conviction of the existence of a God, which they, nevertheless, say is so necessary for all mankind? But can you find any harmony in the theological opinions of the different inspired ones or thinkers scattered over the earth? They themselves, who make a profession of adoring the same God, are they in agreement? Are they content with the proofs that their colleagues bring of his existence? Do they subscribe unanimously to the ideas they present on nature, on his conduct, on the manner of understanding his pretended oracles? Is there a country on earth where the science of God is really perfect? Has this science anywhere taken the consistency and uniformity that we see the science of man assume, even in the most futile crafts, the most despised trades. These words *mind, immateriality, creation, predestination* and *grace;* this mass of subtle distinctions with which theology is everywhere filled; these so ingenious inventions, imagined

by thinkers who have succeeded one another
for so many centuries, have only, alas! confused things all the more, and never has man's
most necessary science, up to this time, ac-
quired the slightest fixity. For thousands of
years the lazy dreamers have perpetually re-
lieved one another to meditate on the Divinity,
to divine his secret will, to invent the proper
hypothesis to develop this important enigma.
Their slight success has not discouraged the
theological vanity: one always speaks of God:
one has his throat cut for God: and this sublime being still remains the most unknown and
the most discussed.

Man would have been too happy, if, limiting
himself to the visible objects which interested
him, he had employed, to perfect his real sci-
ences, his laws, his morals, his education, one-
half the efforts he has put into his researches
on the Divinity. He would have been still
wiser and still more fortunate if he had been
satisfied to let his jobless guides quarrel among
themselves, sounding depths capable of rendering them dizzy, without himself mixing in their
senseless disputes. But it is the essence of
ignorance to attach importance to that which
it does not understand. Human vanity is so
constituted that it stiffens before difficulties.
The more an object conceals itself from our
eyes, the greater the effort we make to seize it,
because it pricks our pride, it excites our cur-
iosity and it appears interesting. In fighting
for his God everyone, in fact, fights only for
the interests of his own vanity, which, of all
the passions produced by the mal-organization

of society, is the quickest to take offense, and the most capable of committing the greatest follies.

If, leaving for a moment the annoying idea that theology gives of a capricious God, whose partial and despotic decrees decide the fate of mankind, we wish to fix our eyes only on the pretended goodness, which all men, even trembling before this God, agree is ascribing to him, if we allow him the purpose that is lent him of having worked only for his own glory, of exacting the homage of intelligent beings; of seeking only in his works the well-being of mankind; how reconcile these views and these dispositions with the ignorance truly invincible in which this God, so glorious and so good, leaves the majority of mankind in regard to God himself? If God wishes to be known, cherished, thanked, why does he not show himself under his favorable features to all these intelligent beings by whom he wishes to be loved and adored? Why not manifest himself to the whole earth in an unequivocal manner, much more capable of convincing us than these private revelations which seem to accuse the Divinity of an annoying partiality for some of his creatures? The all-powerful, should he not have more convincing means by which to show himself to man than these ridiculous metamorphoses, these pretended incarnations, which are attested by writers so little in agreement among themselves? In place of so many miracles, invented to prove the divine mission of so many legislators revered by the different people of the world, the Sovereign of these spirits, could he not convince the human mind in an instant of the things he wished to make known to it? Instead of hanging the sun in the vault of the firmament, instead of scattering stars without order, and the constellations which fill space, would it not have been more in conformity with the views of a God so jealous of his glory and so well-intentioned for mankind, to write, in a manner not subject to dispute, his name, his attributes, his permanent wishes in ineffaceable charactérs, equally understandable to all the inhabitants of the earth? No one would then be able to doubt the existence of God, of his clear will, of his visible intentions. Under the eyes of this so terrible God no one would have the audacity to violate his commands, no mortal would dare risk attracting his anger: finally, no man would have the effrontery to impose on his name or to interpret his will according to his own fancy.

In fact, even while admitting the existence of the theological God, and the reality of his so discordant attributes which they impute to him, one can conclude nothing to authorize the conduct or the cult which one is prescribed to render him. Theology is truly the sieve of the Danaides. By dint of contradictory qualities and hazarded assertions it has, that is to say, so handicapped its God that it has made it impossible for him to act. If he is infinitely good, what reason should we have to fear him? If he is infinitely wise, why should we have doubts concerning our future? If he knows all, why warn him of our needs and fatigue him

with our prayers? If he is everywhere, why
erect temples to him? If he is just, why fear
that he will punish the creatures that he has
filled with weaknesses? If grace does everything for them, what reason would he have for
recompensing them? If he is all-powerful, how
offend him, how resist him? If he is reasonable, how can he be angry at the blind, to whom
he has given the liberty of being unreasonable?
If he is immovable, by what right do we pretend to make him change his decrees? If he
is inconceivable, why occupy ourselves with
him? IF HE HAS SPOKEN, WHY.IS THE
UNIVERSE NOT CONVINCED? If the knowledge of a God is the most necessary, why is it
not the most evident and the clearest.—*Système
de la Nature*. London, 1781.

The enlightened and benevolent Pliny thus
publicly professes himself an atheist:—Qua-
propter effigiem Dei formamque quaerere im-
becillitatis humanae reor.   Quisquis est Deus
(si modo est alius) et quacunque in parte, totus
est sensus, totus est visus, totus auditus, totus
animae, totus animi, totus sui. . . .   Imper-
fectae vero in homine naturæ præcipua solatia
ne deum quidem posse omnia. Namque nec sibi
potest mortem consciscere, si velit, quod homini
dedit optimum in tantis vitae poenis; nec mor-
tales aeternitate donare, aut revocare defunctos;
nec facere ut qui vixit non vixerit, qui honores
gessit non gesserit, nullumque habere in prae-
teritum ius praeterquam oblivionis, atque (ut
facetis quoque argumentis societas haec cum
deo copuletur) ut bis dena viginti non sint, et
multa similiter efficere non posse.—Per quae-

declaratur haud dubie naturae potentiam id quoque esse quod Deum vocamus.—Plin. *Nat. Hist.* cap. de Deo.

The consistent Newtonian is necessarily an atheist. See Sir W. Drummond's *Academical Questions*, chap. iii.—Sir W. seems to consider the atheism to which it leads as a sufficient presumption of the falsehood of the system of gravitation; but surely it is more consistent with the good faith of philosophy to admit a deduction from facts than an hypothesis incapable of proof, although it might militate with the obstinate pre-conceptions of the mob. Had this author, instead of inveighing against the guilt and absurdity of atheism, demonstrated its falsehood, his conduct would have been more suited to the modesty of the skeptic and the toleration of the philosopher.

Omnia enim per Dei potentiam facta sunt: imo quia naturae potentia nulla est nisi ipsa Dei potentia. Certum est nos eatenus Dei potentiam non intelligere, quatenus causas naturales ignoramus; adeoque stulte ad eandem Dei potentiam recurritur, quando rei alicuius causam naturalem, sive est, ipsam Dei potentiam ignoramus.—Spinoza, *Tract. Theologico-Pol.* chap i. p. 14.

ON LIFE

Life and the world, or whatever we call that which we are and feel, is an astonishing thing. The mist of familiarity obscures from us the wonder of our being. We are struck with admiration at some of its transient modifications, but it is itself the great miracle. What are changes of empires, the wreck of dynasties, with the opinions which supported them; what is the birth and the extinction of religious and of political systems, to life? What are the revolutions of the globe which we inhabit, and the operations of the elements of which it is composed, compared with life? What is the universe of stars, and suns, of which this inhabited earth is one, and their motions, and their destiny, compared with life? Life, the great miracle, we admire not, because it is so miraculous. It is well that we are thus shielded by the familiarity of what is at once so certain and so unfathomable, from an astonishment which would otherwise absorb and overawe the functions of that which is its object.

If any artist, I do not say had executed, but had merely conceived in his mind the system of the sun, and the stars, and planets, they not existing, and had painted to us in words, or upon canvas, the spectacle now afforded by the nightly cope of heaven, and illustrated it by the wisdom of astronomy, great would be our admiration. Or had he imagined the scenery of this earth, the mountains, the seas, and the rivers; the grass, and the flowers, and the variety of the forms and masses of the leaves of the woods, and the colors which attend the setting and the rising sun, and the hues of the atmosphere, turbid or serene, these things not before existing, truly we should have been astonished, and it would not have been a vain boast to have said of such a man, "Non merita nome di creatore, se non Iddio ed il Poeta." But now these things are looked on with little wonder, and to be conscious of them with intense delight is esteemed to be the distinguishing mark of a refined and extraordinary person. The multitude of men care not for them. It is thus with Life—that which includes all.

What is life? Thoughts and feelings arise, with or without our will, and we employ words to express them. We are born, and our birth is unremembered, and our infancy remembered but in fragments; we live on, and in living we lose the apprehension of life. How vain is it to think that words can penetrate the mystery of our being! Rightly used they may make evident our ignorance to ourselves; and this is much. For what are we? Whence do we come? and whither do we go? Is birth the commencement, is death the conclusion of our being? What is birth and death?

The most refined abstractions of logic conduct to a view of life, which, though startling to the apprehension, is, in fact, that which the habitual sense of its repeated combinations has extinguished in us. It strips, as it were, the painted curtain from this scene of things. I confess that I am one of those who am unable to refuse my assent to the conclusion of those

philosophers who assert that nothing exists
but as it is perceived.

It is a decision against which all our persua-
sions struggle, and we must be long convicted
before we can be convinced that the solid universe of external things is "such stuff as dreams
are made of." The shocking absurdities of the
popular philosophy of mind and matter, its fatal
consequences in morals, and their violent dog-
matism concerning the source of all things,
had early conducted me to materialism. This
materialism is a seducing system to young and
superficial minds. It allows its disciples to
talk, and dispenses them from thinking. But
I was discontented with such a view of things
as it afforded; man is a being of high aspira-
tions, "looking both before and after," whose
"thoughts wander through eternity," disclaim-
ing alliance with transience and decay; incapable of imagining to himself annihilation; existing but in the future and the past; being,
not what he is, but what he has been and
shall be. Whatever may be his true and final
destination, there is a spirit within him at
enmity with nothingness and dissolution. This
is the character of all life and being. Each is
at once the center and the circumference; the
point to which all things are referred, and the
line in which all things are contained. Such
contemplations as these, materialism and the
popular philosophy of mind and matter alike
forbid; they are only consistent with the intellectual system.

It is absurd to enter into a long recapitula-
tion of arguments sufficiently familiar to those
inquiring minds, whom alone a writer on ab-

struse subjects can be conceived to address.
Perhaps the most clear and vigorous statement
of the intellectual system is to be found in Sir
William Drummond's Academical Questions.
After such an exposition, it would be idle to
tanslate into other words what could only lose
its energy and fitness by the change. Examined
point by point, and word by word, the most dis-
criminating intellects have been able to discern
no train of thoughts in the process of reasoning,
which does not conduct inevitably to the conclusion which has been stated.

What follows from the admission? It establishes no new truth, it gives us no additional
insight into our hidden nature, neither its action nor itself. Philosophy, impatient as it may
be to build, has much work yet remaining as
pioneer for the overgrowth of ages. It makes
one step towards this object; it destroys error,
and the roots of error. It leaves, what it is too
often the duty of the reformer in political and
ethical questions to leave, a vacancy. It re-
duces the mind to that freedom in which it
would have acted, but for the misuse of words
and signs, the instruments of its own creation.
By signs, I would be understood in a wide
sense, including what is properly meant by that
term, and what I peculiarly mean. In this latter sense, almost all familiar objects are signs,
standing, not for themselves, but for others,
in their capacity of suggesting one thought
which shall lead to a train of thoughts. Our
whole life is thus an education of error.

Let us recollect our sensations as children.
What a distinct and intense apprehension had

we of the world and of ourselves! Many of the circumstances of social life were then important to us which are now no longer so. But that is not the point of comparison on which I mean to insist. We less habitually distinguished all that we saw and felt, from ourselves. They seemed, as it were, to constitute one mass. There are some persons who, in this respect, are always children. Those who are subject to the state called reverie, feel as if their nature were dissolved into the surrounding universe, or as if the surrounding universe were absorbed into their being. They are conscious of no distinction. And these are states which precede, or accompany, or follow an unusually intense and vivid apprehension of life. As men grow up this power commonly decays, and they become mechanical and habitual agents. Thus feelings and then reasonings are the combined result of a multitude of entangled thoughts, and of a series of what are called impressions, planted by reiteration.

The view of life presented by the most refined deductions of the intellectual philosophy, is that of unity. Nothing exists but as it is perceived. The difference is merely nominal between those two classes of thought, which are vulgarly distinguished by the names of ideas and of external objects. Pursuing the same thread of reasoning, the existence of distinct individual minds, similar to that which is employed in now questioning its own nature, is likewise found to be a delusion. The words, *I, you, they*, are not signs of any actual difference subsisting between the assemblage of thoughts thus indicated, but are merely marks

employed to denote the different modifications
of the one mind.

Let it not be supposed that this doctrine
conducts the monstrous presumption that I, the
person who now write and think, am that one
mind. I am but a portion of it. The words *I*,
and *you*, and *they* are grammatical devices invented simply for arrangement, and totally de-
void of the intense and exclusive sense usually
attached to them. It is difficult to find terms
adequate to express so subtle a conception as
that to which the Intellectual Philosophy has
conducted us. We are on that verge where
words abandon us, and what wonder if we grow
dizzy to look down the dark abyss of how little we know!

The relations of *things* remain unchanged, by
whatever system. By the word *things* is to be
understood any object of thought, that is, any
thought upon which any other thought is employed, with an apprehension of distinction.
The relations of these remain unchanged; and
such is. the material of our knowledge.

What is the cause of life? that is, how was
it produced, or what agencies distinct from life
have acted or act upon life? All recorded gen-
erations of mankind have wearily busied themselves in inventing answers to this question;
and the result has been—Religion. Yet that the
basis of all things cannot be, as the popular
philosophy alleges, mind, is sufficiently evident.
Mind, as far as we have any experience of its
properties—and beyond that experience how
vain is argument!—cannot create, it can only
perceive. It is said also to be the cause. But
cause is only a word expressing a certain state

of the human mind with regard to the manner in which two thoughts are apprehended to be related to each other. If anyone desires to know how unsatisfactorily the popular philosophy employs itself upon this great question, they need only impartially reflect upon the manner in which thoughts develop themselves in their minds. It is infinitely improbable that the cause of mind, that is, of existence, is similar to mind.

ON A FUTURE STATE

It has been the persuasion of an immense majority of human beings in all ages and nations that we continue to live after death—that apparent termination of all the functions of sensitive and intellectual existence. Nor has mankind been contented with supposing that species of existence which some philosophers have asserted; namely, the resolution of the component parts of the mechanism of a living being into its elements, and the impossibility of the minutest particle of these sustaining the smallest diminution. They have clung to the idea that sensibility and thought, which they have distinguished from the objects of it, under the several names of spirit and matter, is, in its own nature, less susceptible of division and decay, and that, when the body is resolved into its elements, the principle which animated it will remain perpetual and unchanged. Some philosophers—and those to whom we are indebted for the most stupendous discoveries in physical science—suppose, on the other hand, that intelligence is the mere result of certain combinations among the particles of its objects; and those among them who believe that we live after death, recur to the interposition of a supernatural power, which shall overcome the tendency inherent in all material combinations, to dissipate and be absorbed into other forms.

Let us trace the reasonings which in one and the other have conducted to these two opinions, and endeavor to discover what we ought to think on a question of such momentous interest. Let us analyze the ideas and feelings which constitute the contending beliefs, and watchfully establish a discrimination between words and thoughts. Let us bring the question to the test of experience and fact; and ask ourselves, considering our nature in its entire extent, what light we derive from a sustained and comprehensive view of its component parts, which may enable us to assert, with certainty, that we do or do not live after death.

The examination of this subject requires that it should be stripped of all those accessory topics which adhere to it in the common opinion of men. The existence of a God, and a future state of rewards and punishments are totally foreign to the subject. If it be proved that the world is ruled by a Divine Power, no inference necessarily can be drawn from that circumstance in favor of a future state. It has been asserted, indeed, that as goodness and justice are to be numbered among the attributes of the Deity, he will undoubtedly compensate the virtuous who suffer during life, and that he will make every sensitive being, who does not deserve punishment, happy forever. But this view of the subject, which it would be tedious as well as superfluous to develop and expose, satisfies no person, and cuts the knot which we now seek to untie. Moreover, should it be proved, on the other hand, that the mysterious principle which regulates the proceedings of the universe, is neither intelligent nor sensitive, yet it is not an inconsistency to suppose at the same time, that the animating power survives the body which it has animated, by laws as independent of any supernatural agent as those through which it first became

united with it. Nor, if a future state be clearly
proved, does it follow that it will be a state of
punishment or reward.

By the word death, we express that condition
in which natures resembling ourselves apparently cease to be that which they are. We no
longer hear them speak, nor see them move.
If they have sensations and apprehensions, we
no longer participate in them. We know no
more than that those external organs, and all
that fine texture of material frame, without
which we have no experience that life or
thought can subsist, are dissolved and scattered
abroad. The body is placed under the earth,
and after a certain period there remains no
vestige even of its form. This is that contemplation of inexhaustible melancholy, whose
shadow eclipses the brightness of the world.
The common observer is struck with dejection
of the spectacle. He contends in vain against
the persuasion of the grave, that the dead indeed cease to be. The corpse at his feet is
prophetic of his own destiny. Those who have
preceded him, and whose voice was delightful
to his ear; whose touch met his like sweet and
subtle fire; whose aspect spread a visionary
light upon his path—these he cannot meet
again. The organs of sense are destroyed, and
the intellectual operations dependent on them
have perished with their sources. How can a
corpse see or feel? its eyes are eaten out, and
its heart is black and without motion. What
intercourse can two heaps of putrid clay and
crumbling bones hold together? When you
can discover where the fresh colors of the
faded flower abide, or the music of the broken

lyre, seek life among the dead. Such are the anxious and fearful contemplations of the common observer, though the popular religion often prevents him from confessing them even to himself.

The natural philosopher, in addition to the sensations common to all men inspired by the event of death, believes that he sees with more certainty that it is attended with the annihilation of sentiment and thought. He observes the mental powers increase and fade with those of the body, and even accommodate themselves to the most transitory changes of our physical nature. Sleep suspends many of the faculties of the vital and intellectual principle; drunkenness and disease will either temporarily or permanently derange them. Madness or idiocy may utterly extinguish the most excellent and delicate of those powers. In old age the mind gradually withers; and as it grew and was strengthened with the body, so does it together with the body sink into decrepitude. Assuredly these are convincing evidences that so soon as the organs of the body are subjected to the laws of inanimate matter, sensation, and perception, and apprehension, are at an end. It is probable that what we call thought is not an actual being, but no more than the relation between certain parts of that infinitely varied mass, of which the rest of the universe is composed, and which ceases to exist so soon as those parts change their position with regard to each other. Thus color, and sound, and taste, and odor exist only relatively. But let thought be considered as some peculiar substance, which permeates, and is the cause of, the animation of living beings. Why should that substance be as-

sumed to be something essentially distinct from
all others, and exempt from subjection to those
laws from which no other substance is exempt?
It differs, indeed, from all other substances, as
electricity, and light, and magnetism, and the
constituent parts of air and earth, severally differ from all others. Each of these is subject to
change and to decay, and to conversion into
other forms. Yet the difference between light
and earth is scarcely greater than that which
exists between life, or thought, and fire. The
difference between the two former was never
alleged as an argument for the eternal perma-
nence of either, in that form under which they
first might offer themselves to our notice. Why
should the difference between the two latter
substances be an argument for the prolonga-
tion of the existence of one and not the other,
when the existence of both has arrived at their
apparent termination? To say that fire exists
without manifesting any of the properties of
fire, such as light, heat, etc., or that the principle of life exists without consciousness, or
memory, or desire, or motive, is to resign, by
an awkward distortion of language, the affirmative of the dispute. To say that the principle
of life *may* exist in distribution among various forms, is to assert what cannot be proved
to be either true or false, but which, were it
true, annihilates all hope of existence after
death, in any sense in which that event can
belong to the hopes and fears of men. Suppose,
however, that the intellectual and vital principle differs in the most marked and essential
manner from all other known substances; that
they have all some resemblance between them-

selves which it in no degree participates. In what manner can this concession be made an argument for its imperishability? All that we see or know perishes and is changed. Life and thought differ indeed from everything else. But that it survives that period, beyond which we have no experience of its existence, such distinction and dissimilarity affords no shadow of proof, and nothing but our own desires could have led us to conjecture or imagine.

Have we existed before birth? It is difficult to conceive the possibility of this. There is, in the generative principle of each animal and plant, a power which converts the substances by which it is surrounded into a substance homogeneous with itself. That is, the relations between certain elementary particles of matter undergo a change, and submit to new combinations. For when we use words *principle, power, cause,* etc., we mean to express no real being, but only to class under those terms a certain series of coexisting phenomena; but let it be supposed that this principle is a certain substance which escapes the observation of the chemist and anatomist. It certainly *may be;* though it is sufficiently unphilosophical to allege the possibility of an opinion as a proof of its truth. Does it see, hear, feel, before its combination with those organs on which sensation depends? Does it reason, imagine, apprehend, without those ideas which sensation alone can communicate? If we have not existed before birth; if, at the period when the parts of our nature on which thought and life depend, seem to be woven together, they are woven together; if there are no reasons to suppose that we have

existed before that period at which our existence apparently commences, then there are no
grounds for supposition that we shall continue
to exist after our existence has apparently
ceased. So far as thought and life is concerned,
the same will take place with regard to us, in-
dividually considered, after death, as had place
before our birth.

It is said that it is possible that we should
continue to exist in some mode totally inconceivable to us at present. This is a most unreasonable presumption. It casts on the adherents of annihilation the burthen of proving
the negative of a question, the affirmative of
which is not supported by a single argument,
and which, by its very nature, lies beyond the
experience of the human understanding. It is
sufficiently easy, indeed, to form any proposition, concerning which we are ignorant, just not
so absurd as not to be contradictory in itself,
and defy refutation. The possibility of whatever enters into the wildest imagination to
conceive is thus triumphantly vindicated. But
it is enough that such assertions should be
either contradictory to the known laws of nature, or exceed the limits of our experience,
that their fallacy or irrelevancy to our consideration should be demonstrated. They persuade, indeed, only those who desire to be per-
suaded.

This desire to be forever as we are; the re-
luctance to a violent and unexperienced change,
which is common to all the animated and inanimate combinations of the universe, is, indeed, the secret persuasion which has given
birth to the opinions of a future state.

A REFUTATION OF DEISM

EUSEBES AND THEOSOPHUS

[This discussion is in the form of a rational
dialogue between Eusebes, who supports Christianity, and Theosophus, who is a skeptic.
Eusebes opens with a long preamble, summariz-
ing various claims to support the validity of his
belief: the ancient books predicting the Messiah,
the suffering of martyrs in the name of their
faith, the miraculous history of the progress of
Christianity, the moral tenets of the faith, the
intervention of God to save mankind, He urges
Theosophus to consider the curses and punishments heaped upon the unbeliever. Whereupon,
Theosophus proceeds to reply, to explain his
skepticism.]

I am not only prepared to confess, but to vindicate my sentiments. I cannot refrain, however, from premising, that in this controversy
I labor under a disadvantage from which you
are exempt. You believe that incredulity is
immoral, and regard him as an object of suspicion and distrust whose creed is incongruous
with your own. But truth is the perception
of the agreement or disagreement of ideas. I
can no more conceive that a man who perceives
the disagreement of any ideas should be per-
suaded of their agreement, than that he should
overcome a physical impossibility. The reason-
ableness or the folly of the articles of our creed
is therefore no legitimate object of merit or
demerit; our opinions depend not on the will,
but on the understanding.

If I am in error (and the wisest of us may
not presume to deem himself secure from all
illusion) that error is the consequence of the
prejudices by which I am prevented, of the
ignorance by which I am incapacitated from

forming a correct estimation of the subject. Remove those prejudices, dispel that ignorance, make truth apparent, and fear not the obstacles that remain to be encountered. But do not repeat to me those terrible and frequent curses, by whose intolerance and cruelty I have so often been disgusted in the perusal of your sacred books. Do not tell me that the All-Merciful will punish me for the conclusions of that reason by which he has thought fit to distinguish me from the beasts that perish. Above all, refrain from urging considerations drawn from reason, to degrade that which you are thereby compelled to acknowledge as the ultimate arbiter of the dispute. Answer my objections as I engage to answer your assertions, point by point, word by word.

You believe that the only and ever-present God begot a Son whom he sent to reform the world, and to propitiate its sins; you believe that a book, called the Bible, contains a true account of this event, together with an infinity of miracles and prophecies which preceded it from the creation of the world. Your opinion that these circumstances really happened appears to me, from some considerations which I will proceed to state, destitute of rational foundation.

To expose all the inconsistency, immorality and false pretensions which I perceive in the Bible, demands a minuteness of criticism at least as voluminous as itself. I shall confine myself, therefore, to the confronting of your tenets with those primitive and general principles which are the basis of all moral reasoning.

In creating the Universe, God certainly proposed to himself the happiness of his creatures. It is just, therefore, to conclude that he left no means unemployed, which did not involve an impossibility, to accomplish this design. In fixing a residence for this image of his own Majesty, he was doubtless careful that every occasion of detriment, every opportunity of evil, should be removed. He was aware of the extent of his powers, he foresaw the consequences of his conduct, and doubtless modeled his being consentaneously with the world of which he was to be inhabitant, and the circumstances which were destined to surround him.

The account given by the Bible has but a faint concordance with the surmises of reason concerning this event.

According to this book, God created Satan, who, instigated by the impulses of his nature, contended with the Omnipotent for the throne of Heaven. After a contest for the empire, in which God was victorious, Satan was thrust into a pit of burning sulphur. On man's creation, God placed within his reach a tree whose fruit he forbade him to taste, on pain of death; permitting Satan, at the same time, to employ all his artifice to persuade this innocent and wondering creature to transgress the fatal prohibition.

The first man yielded to this temptation; and to satisfy Divine Justice the whole of his posterity must have been eternally burned in hell, if God had not sent his only Son on earth, to save those few whose salvation had been foreseen and determined before the creation of the world.

God is here represented as creating man with certain passions and powers, surrounding him with certain circumstances, and then condemning him to everlasting torments because he acted as Omniscience had foreseen, and was such as Omnipotence had made him. For to assert that the Creator is the author of all good, and the creature the author of all evil, is to assert that one man makes a straight line and a crooked one, and that another makes the incongruity.

Barbarous and uncivilized nations have uniformly adored, under various names, a God of which themselves were the model: revengeful, blood-thirsty, groveling and capricious. The steam of slaughter, the dissonance of groans, the flames of a desolated land, are the offerings which he deems acceptable, and his innumerable votaries throughout the world have made it a point of duty to worship him to his taste. The Phenicians, the Druids and the Mexicans have immolated hundreds at the shrines of their divinity, and the high and holy name of God has been in all ages the watchword of the most unsparing massacres, the sanction of the most atrocious perfidies.

But I appeal to your candor, O Eusebes, if there exist a record of such groveling absurdities and enormities so atrocious, a picture of the Deity so characteristic of a demon as that which the sacred writings of the Jews contain. I demand of you, whether as a conscientious Theist you can reconcile the conduct which is attributed to the God of the Jews with your conceptions of the purity and benevolence of the divine nature.

The loathsome and minute obscenities to which the inspired writers perpetually descend, the filthy observances which God is described as personally instituting, the total disregard of truth and contempt of the first principles of morality, manifested on the most public occasions by the chosen favorites of Heaven, might corrupt, were they not so flagitious as to disgust.

When the chief of this obscure and brutal horde of assassins assert that the God of the Universe was enclosed in a box of shittim

wood, "two feet long and three feet wide,"
and brought home in a new cart, I smile at
the impertinence of so shallow an imposture.
But it is blasphemy of a more hideous and unexampled nature to maintain that the Almighty
God expressly commanded Moses to invade an
unoffending nation; and, on account of the difference of their worship, utterly to destroy
every human being it contained, to murder
every infant and unarmed man in cold blood,
to massacre the captives, to rip up the matrons,
and retain the maidens alone for concubinage
and violation. At the very time that philosophers of the most enterprising benevolence
were founding in Greece those institutions
which have rendered it the wonder and lumi-
nary of the world, am I required to believe
that the weak and wicked king of an obscure
and barbarous nation, a murderer, a traitor and
a tyrant, was the man after God's own heart?
A wretch, at the thought of whose unparalleled
enormities the sternest soul must sicken in
dismay! An unnatural monster, who sawed his
fellow beings in sunder, harrowed them to
fragments under harrows of iron, chopped them
to pieces with axes, and burned them in brick-
kilns, because they bowed before a different,
and less bloody idol than his own. It is surely
no perverse conclusion of an infatuated understanding that the God of the Jews is not the
benevolent author of this beautiful world.*

The conduct of the Deity in the promulgation
of the Gospel, appears not to the eye of reason
more compatible with his immutability and
omnipotence than the history of his actions under the law accords with his benevolence.

You assert that the human race merited eter-

---

*Ex. 32, 26; Num. 31, 7-18; Deut. 3, 6; Joshua
10; 2 Sam. 12, 29.

nal reprobation because their common father
had transgressed the divine command, and that
the crucifixion of the Son of God was the only
sacrifice or sufficient efficacy to satisfy eternal
justice. But it is no less inconsistent with justice and subversive of morality that millions
should be responsible for a crime which they
had no share in committing, than that, if they
had really committed it, the crucifixion of an
innocent being could absolve them from moral
turpitude. Certainly this is a mode of legislation peculiar to a state of savageness and an-
archy; this is the irrefragable logic of tyranny
and imposture.

The supposition that God has never supernat-
urally revealed his will to man at any other
period than the original creation of the human
race, necessarily involves a compromise of his
benevolence. It assumes that he withheld from
mankind a benefit which it was in his power to
confer. That he suffered his creatures to remain in ignorance of truths essential to their
happiness and salvation. That during the lapse
of innumerable ages, every individual of the
human race had perished without redemption,
from an universal stain which the Deity at
length descended in person to erase. That the
good and wise of all ages, involved in one common fate with the ignorant and wicked, have
been tainted by involuntary and inevitable
error which torments infinite in duration may
not avail to expiate.

In vain will you assure me with amiable inconsistency that the mercy of God will be extended to the virtuous, and that the vicious
will alone be punished. The foundation of the
Christian Religion is manifestly compromised
by a concession of this nature. A subterfuge
thus palpable plainly annihilates the necessity
of the incarnation of God for the redemption

of the human race, and represents the descent of the Messiah as a gratuitous display of Deity, solely adapted to perplex, to terrify and to embroil mankind.

It is sufficiently evident that an omniscient being never conceived the design of reforming the world by Christianity. Omniscience would surely have foreseen the inefficacy of that system, which experience demonstrates not only to have been utterly impotent in restraining, but to have been most active in exhaling the malevolent propensities of men. During the period which elapsed between the removal of the seat of empire to Constantinople in 328, and its capture by the Turks in 1453, what salutary influence did Christianity exercise upon that world which it was intended to enlighten? Never before was Europe the theater of such ceaseless and sanguinary wars; never were the people so brutalized by ignorance and debased by slavery.

I will admit that one prediction of Jesus Christ has been indisputably fulfilled. *I come not to bring peace upon earth, but a sword.* Christianity indeed has equalled Judaism in the atrocities, and exceeded it in the extent of its desolation. Eleven millions of men, women, and children, have been killed in battle, butchered in their sleep, burned to death at public festivals of sacrifice, poisoned, tortured, assassinated, and pillaged in the spirit of the Religion of Peace, and for the glory of the most merciful God.

In vain will you tell me that these terrible effects flow not from Christianity, but from the abuse of it. No such excuse will avail to palliate the enormities of a religion pretended to be divine. A limited intelligence is only so far responsible for the effects of its agency as it foresaw, or might have foreseen them; but

Omniscience is manifestly chargeable with all the consequences of its conduct. Christianity itself declares that the worth of the tree is to be determined by the quality of its fruit. The extermination of infidels; the mutual persecutions of hostile sects; the midnight massacres and slow burning of thousands, because their creed contained either more or less than the orthodox standard, of which Christianity has been the immediate occasion; and the invariable opposition which philosophy has ever encountered from the spirit of revealed religion, plainly show that a very slight portion of sagacity was sufficient to have estimated at its true value the advantages of that belief to which some Theists are unaccountably attached.

You lay great stress upon the originality of the Christian system of morals. If this claim be just, either your religion must be false, or the Deity has willed that opposite modes of conduct should be pursued by mankind at different times, under the same circumstances; which is absurd.

The doctrine of acquiescing in the most insolent despotism; of praying for and loving our enemies; of faith and humility, appears to fix the perfection of the human character in that abjectness and credulity which priests and tyrants of all ages have found sufficiently convenient for their purposes. It is evident that a whole nation of Christians (such such an anomaly maintain itself a day) would become, like cattle, the property of the first occupier. It is evident that ten highwaymen would suffice to subjugate the world if it were composed of slaves who dared not to resist oppression.

The apathy to love and friendship, recommended by your creed, would, if attainable, not be less pernicious. This enthusiasm of anti-social misanthropy, if it were an actual rule of conduct, and not the speculation of a few interested persons, would speedily annihilate the human race. A total abstinence from sexual intercourse is not perhaps enjoined, but is strenuously recommended, and was actually practiced to a frightful extent by the primitive Christians.

The penalties inflicted by that monster Constantine, the first Christian Emperor, on the pleasures of unlicensed love, are so iniquitously severe, that no modern legislator could have affixed them to the most atrocious crimes. This cold-blooded and hypocritical ruffian cut his son's throat, strangled his wife, murdered his father-in-law and his brother-in-law, and maintained at his court a set of blood-thirsty and bigoted Christian Priests, one of whom was sufficient to excite the one-half of the world to massacre the other.

I am willing to admit that some few axioms of morality, which Christianity has borrowed from the philosophers of Greece and India, dictate, in an unconnected state, rules of conduct worthy of regard; but the purest and most elevated lessons of morality must remain nugatory, the most probable inducements to virtue must fail of their effect, so long as the slightest weight is attached to that dogma which is the vital essence of revealed religion.

Belief is set up as the criterion of merit or demerit; a man is to be judged not by the purity of his intentions but by the orthodoxy of his creed; an assent to certain propositions, is to outweigh in the balance of Christianity the most generous and elevated virtue.

But the intensity of belief, like that of every other passion, is precisely proportioned to the degrees of excitement. A graduated scale, on which should be marked the capabilities of propositions to approach to the test of the senses, would be a just measure of the belief which ought to be attached to them: and but for the influence of prejudice or ignorance this invariably *is* the measure of belief. That is believed which is apprehended to be true, nor can the mind by any exertion avoid attaching credit to an opinion attended with overwhelming evidence. Belief is not an act of volition, nor can it be regulated by the mind: it is manifestly incapable therefore of either merit or criminality. The system which assumes a false criterion of moral virtue, must be as pernicious as it is absurd. Above all, it cannot be divine, as it is impossible that the Creator of the human mind should be ignorant of its primary powers.

The degree of evidence afforded by miracles and prophecies in favor of the Christian Religion is lastly to be considered.

Evidence of a more imposing and irresistible nature is required in proportion to the remoteness of any event from the sphere of our experience. Every case of miracles is a contest of opposite improbabilities, whether it is more contrary to experience that a miracle should be true, or that the story on which it is supported should be false: whether the immutable laws of this harmonious world should have undergone violation, or that some obscure Greeks and Jews should have conspired to fabricate a tale of wonder.

The actual appearance of a departed spirit would be a circumstance truly unusual and portentous; but the accumulated testimony of twelve old women that a spirit had appeared is neither unprecedented nor miraculous.

It seems less credible that the God whose immensity is uncircumscribed by space, should have committed adultery with a carpenter's

wife, than that some bold knaves or insane
dupes had deceived the credulous multitude.
We have perpetual and mournful experience
of the latter: the former is yet under dispute.
History affords us innumerable examples of
the possibility of the one: Philosophy has in
all ages protested the probability of the other.

Every superstition can produce its dupes, its
miracles, and its mysteries; each is prepared
to justify its peculiar tenets by an equal assemblage of portents, prophecies and martyr-
doms.

Prophecies, however circumstantial, are lia-
ble to the same objection as direct miracles:
it is more agreeable to experience that the
historical evidence of the prediction really
having preceded the event pretended to be
foretold should be false, or that a lucky con-
juncture of events should have justified the
conjecture of the prophet, than that God should
communicate to a man the discernment of
future events. I defy you to produce more
than one instance of prophecy in the Bible,
wherein the inspired writer speaks so as to be
understood, wherein his prediction has not
been so unintelligible and obscure as to have
been itself the subject of controversy among
Christians.

That one prediction which I except is certainly most explicit and circumstantial. It is
the only one of this nature which the Bible
contains. Jesus himself here predicts his own
arrival in the clouds to consummate a period
of supernatural desolation, before the generation which he addressed should pass away.
Eighteen hundred years have past, and no such
event is pretended to have happened. This
single plain prophecy, thus conspicuously
false, may serve as a criterion of those which

are more vague and indirect, and which apply in an hundred senses to an hundred things.

Either the pretended predictions in the Bible were meant to be understood, or they were not. If they were, why is there any dispute concerning them: if they were not, wherefore were they written at all? But the God of Christianity spoke to mankind in parables, that seeing they might not see, and hearing they might not understand.

The Gospels contain internal evidence that they were not written by eye-witnesses of the event which they pretend to record. The Gospel of St. Matthew was plainly not written until some time after the taking of Jerusalem, that is, at least forty years after the execution of Jesus Christ: for he makes Jesus say that *upon you may come all the righteous blood shed upon the earth, from the blood of righteous Abel unto the blood of Zacharias son of Barachias whom ye slew between the altar and the temple.* Now Zacharias, son of Barachias, was assassinated between the altar and the temple by a faction of zealots, during the siege of Jerusalem.

You assert that the design of the instances of supernatural interposition which the Gospel records was to convince mankind that Jesus Christ was truly the expected Redeemer. But it is as impossible that any human sophistry should frustrate the manifestation of Omnipotence, as that Omniscience should fail to select the most efficient means of accomplishing its design. Eighteen centuries have passed and the tenth part of the human race have a blind and mechanical belief in that Redeemer, without a complete reliance on the merits of whom, their lot is fixed in everlasting misery:

surely if the Christian system be thus dreadfully important its Omnipotent author would have rendered it incapable of those abuses from which it has never been exempt, and to which it is subject in common with all human institutions, he would not have left it a matter of ceaseless cavil or complete indifference to the immense majority of mankind. Surely some more conspicuous evidences of its authenticity would have been afforded than driving out devils, drowning pigs, curing blind men, animating a dead body, and turning water into wine. Some theater worthier of the transcendent event, than Judea, would have been chosen, some historians more adapted by their accomplishments and their genius to record the incarnation of the immutable God. The humane society restores drowned persons; every empiric can cure every disease; drowning pigs is no very difficult matter, and driving out devils was far from being an original or an unusual occupation in Judea. Do not recite these stale absurdities as proofs of the Divine origin of Christianity.

If the Almighty has spoken, would not the Universe have been convinced? If he had judged the knowledge of his will to have been more important than any other science to mankind, would he not have rendered it more evident and more clear?

Now, O Eusebes, have I enumerated the general grounds of my disbelief of the Christian Religion.—I could have collated its Sacred Writings with the Brahminical record of the early ages of the world, and identified its institutions with the ancient worship of the Sun. I might have entered into an elaborate comparison of the innumerable discordances which exist between the inspired historians of the same event. Enough however has been said to vindicate me from the charge of groundless was infatuated skepticism. I trust therefore to your candor for the consideration, and to your logic for the refutation, of my arguments.

EUSEBES

I will not dissemble, O Theosophus, the difficulty of solving your general objections to Christianity, on the grounds of human reason. I did not assist at the councils of the Almighty when he determined to extend his mercy to mankind, nor can I venture to affirm that it exceeded the limits of his power to have afforded a more conspicuous or universal manifestation of his will.

But this is a difficulty which attends Christianity in common with the belief in the being and attributes of God. This whole scheme of things might have been, according to our partial conceptions, infinitely more admirable and perfect. Poisons, earthquakes, disease, war, famine and venomous serpents; slavery and persecution are the consequences of certain causes, which according to human judgment might well have been dispensed with in arranging the economy of the globe.

Is this the reasoning which the Theist will choose to employ? Will he impose limitations on that Deity whom he professes to regard with so profound a veneration? Will he place his God between the horns of a logical dilemma which shall restrict the fulness either of his power or his bounty?

Certainly he will prefer to resign his objections to Christianity, than pursue the reasoning upon which they are found, to the dreadful conclusions of cold and dreary Atheism.

[Eusebes protests that reason is likely, as used by Theosophus, to take all good and happiness from humanity, and urge that Christianity is preferable to Atheism. Theosophus admits this for the Atheist is obviously a law unto himself—"he is not to be restrained by punishments, for death is divested of its terror, and whatever enters into his heart to conceive, that will he not scruple to execute." The universe does have a design, he says, which establishes a designer. Theosophus agrees, then, to reject reason is Eusebes will demonstrate that it leads to Atheism. So Eusebes requests that Theosophus state his reasons for a belief in God, and he, if his argumentary blasphemy may be pardoned, will contradict those reasons by reason itself thus showing the dangers of rationalism!]

THEOSOPHUS

I will readily state the grounds of my belief in the being of a God. You can only have remained ignorant of the obvious proofs of this important truth, from a superstitious reliance upon the evidence afforded by a revealed religion. The reasoning lies within an extremely narrow compass.

From every design we justly infer a designer. If we examine the structure of a watch, we shall readily confess the existence of a watchmaker. No work of man could possibly have existed from all eternity. From the contemplation of any product of human art, we conclude that there was an artificer who arranged its several parts. In like manner, from the marks of design and contrivance exhibited in the Universe, we are necessitated to infer a designer, a contriver. If the parts of the Universe have been designed, contrived, and adapted, the existence of a God is manifest.

But design is sufficiently apparent. The wonderful adaptation of substances which act

to those which are acted upon; of the eye to
light, and of light to the eye; of the ear to
sound, and of sound to the ear; of every object of sensation to the sense which it im-
presses prove that neither blind chance, nor
undistinguishing necessity has brought them
into being. The adaptation of certain animals
to certain climates, the relation borne to each
other by animals and vegetables, and by different tribes of animals; the relation, lastly,
between man and the circumstances of his external situation are so many demonstrations of
Deity.

All is order, design, and harmony, so far as
we can descry the tendency of things, and
every new enlargement of our views, every
new display of the material world, affords a
new illustration of the power, the wisdom and
the benevolence of God.

The existence of God has never been the
topic of popular dispute. There is a tendency
to devotion, a thirst for reliance on supernatural aid inherent in the human mind.
Scarcely any people, however barbarous, have
been discovered, who do not acknowledge with
reverence and awe the supernatural causes of
the natural effects which they experience.
They worship, it is true, the vilest and most
inanimate substances, but they firmly confide
in the holiness and power of these symbols,
and thus own their connection with what they
can neither see nor perceive.

If there is motion in the Universe, there is
a God. The power of beginning motion is no
less an attribute of mind than sensation or
thought. Wherever motion exists it is evident
that mind has operated. The phenomena of
the Universe indicate the agency of powers
which cannot belong to inert matter.

Every thing which begins to exist must have

a cause: every combination, conspired to an end, implies intelligence.

EUSEBES

Design must be proved before a designer can be inferred. The matter in controversy is the existence of design in the Universe, and it is not permitted to assume the contested premises and thence infer the matter in dispute. Insidiously to employ the words contrivance, design, and adaptation before these circumstances are made apparent in the Universe, thence justly inferring a contriver, is a popular sophism against which it behooves us to be watchful.

To assert that motion is an attribute of mind, that matter is inert, that every combination is the result of intelligence is also an assumption of the matter in dispute.

Why do we admit design in any machine of human contrivance? Simply because innumerable instances of machines having been contrived by human art are present to our mind, because we are acquainted with persons who could construct such machines; but if, having no previous knowledge of any artificial contrivance, we had accidentally found a watch upon the ground, we should have been justified in concluding that it was a thing of Nature, that it was a combination of matter with whose cause we were unacquainted, and that any attempt to account for the origin of its existence would be equally presumptuous and unsatisfactory.

The analogy which you attempt to establish between the contrivances of human art, and the various existences of the Universe, is inadmissible. We attribute these effects to human intelligence, because we know beforehand that human intelligence is capable of producing them. Take away this knowledge, and the grounds of our reasoning will be destroyed. Our entire ignorance, therefore, of the Divine Nature leaves this analogy defective in its most essential point of comparison.

What consideration remains to be urged in support of the creation of the Universe by a supreme Being? Its admirable fitness for the production of certain effects, that wonderful consent of all its parts, that universal harmony by whose changeless laws innumerable systems of worlds perform their stated revolutions, and the blood is driven through the veins of the minutest animalcule that sports in the corruption of an insect's lymph: on this account did the Universe require an intelligent Creator, because it exists producing invariable effects, and inasmuch as it is admirably organized for the production of these effects, so the more did it require a creative intelligence.

Thus have we arrived at the substance of your assertion, "That whatever exists, producing certain effects, stands in need of a Creator, and the more conspicuous is its fitness for the production of these effects, the more certain will be our conclusion that it would not have existed from eternity, but must have derived its origin from an intelligent creator."

In what respect then do these arguments apply to the Universe, and not apply to God? From the fitness of the Universe to its end you infer the necessity of an intelligent Creator. But if the fitness of the Universe, to produce certain effects, be thus conspicuous and evident, how much more exquisite fitness to his end must exist in the Author of this Universe? If we find great difficulty from its admirable arrangement in conceiving that the Universe has existed from all eternity, and to resolve this difficulty suppose a Creator, how much more clearly must we perceive the necessity of this very Creator's creation whose perfections comprehend an arrangement far more accurate and just.

The belief of an infinity of creative and created Gods, each more eminently requiring an intelligent author of his being than the foregoing, is a direct consequence of the premises which you have stated. The assumption that the Universe is a design, leads to a conclusion that there are [an] infinity of creative and created Gods, which is absurd. It is impossible indeed to prescribe limits to learned error, when Philosophy relinquishes experience and feeling for speculation.

Until it is clearly proved that the Universe was created, we may reasonably suppose that it has endured from all eternity. In a case where two propositions are diametrically opposite, the mind believes that which is less incomprehensible: it is easier to suppose that the Universe has existed from all eternity, than to conceive an eternal being capable of creating it. If the mind sinks beneath the weight of one, is it an alleviation to increase the intolerability of the burthen?

A man knows, not only that he now is, but that there was a time when he did not exist; consequently there must have been a cause. But we can only infer, from effects, causes exactly adequate to those effects. There certainly is a generative power which is effected by particular instruments; we cannot prove that it is inherent in these instruments, nor is the contrary hypothesis capable of demonstration. We admit that the generative power is incomprehensible, but to suppose that the same effects are produced by an eternal Omnipotent and Omniscient Being leaves the cause in the same obscurity, but renders it more incomprehensible.

We can only infer from effects causes exactly adequate to those effects. An infinite number of effects demand an infinite number of causes, nor is the philosopher justified in supposing a greater connection or unity in the latter, than is perceptible in the former. The same energy cannot be at once the cause of the serpent and the sheep; of the blight by which the harvest is destroyed, and the sunshine by which it is matured; of the ferocious propensities by which man becomes a victim to himself, and of the accurate judgment by which his institutions are improved. The spirit of our accurate and exact philosophy is outraged by conclusions which contradict each other so glaringly.

The greatest, equally with the smallest motions of the Universe, are subjected to the rigid necessity of inevitable laws. These laws are the unknown causes of the known effects perceivable in the Universe. Their effects are the boundaries of our knowledge, their names the expressions of our ignorance. To suppose some existence beyond, or above them, is to invent a second and superfluous hypothesis to account for what has already been accounted for by the laws of motion and the properties of matter. I admit that the nature of these laws is incomprehensible, but the hypothesis of a Deity adds a gratuitous difficulty, which so far from alleviating those which it is adduced to explain, requires new hypothesis for the elucidation of its own inherent contradictions.

The laws of attraction and repulsion, desire and aversion, suffice to account for every phenomenon of the moral and physical world. A precise knowledge of the properties of any object, is alone requisite to determine its manner of action. Let the mathematician be acquainted with the weight and volume of a cannon ball, together with the degree of velocity and inclination with which it is impelled, and he will accurately delineate the course it must describe, and determine the force with which it will strike an object at a given distance. Let the influencing motive, present to the mind of any person be given, and the knowledge of his consequent conduct will result. Let the bulk and velocity of a comet be discovered, and the astronomer, by the accurate estimation of the equal and contrary actions of the centripetal and centrifugal forces, will justly predict the period of its return.

The anomalous motions of the heavenly bodies, their unequal velocities and frequent aberrations, are corrected by that gravitation by which they are caused. The illustrious Laplace has shown that the approach of the Moon to the Earth, and the Earth to the Sun, is only a secular equation of a very long period, which has its maximum and minimum. The system of the Universe then is upheld solely by physical powers. The necessity of matter is the ruler of the world. It is vain philosophy which supposes more causes than are exactly adequate to explain the phenomena of things.

You assert that the construction of the animal machine, the fitness of certain animals to certain situations, the connection between the organs of perception and that which is perceived; the relation between everything which exists, and that which tends to preserve it in its existence, imply design. It is manifest that if the eye could not see, nor the stomach digest, the human frame could not preserve its present mode of existence. It is equally certain, however, that the elements of its composition, if they did not exist in one form, must exist in another; and that the combinations which they would form, must so long as they endured, derive support for their peculiar mode of being from this fitness to the circumstances of their situation.

It by no means follows, that because a being exists, preforming certain functions, he was fitted by another being to the performances of these functions. So rash a conclusion would conduct, as I have before shown, to an absurdity; and it becomes infinitely more unwarrantable from the consideration that the known laws of matter and motion, suffice to unravel, even in the present imperfect state of moral and physical science, the majority of those difficulties which the hypothesis of a Deity was invented to explain.

Doubtless no disposition of inert matter, or matter deprived of qualities, could ever have composed an animal, a tree, or even a stone. But matter deprived of qualities, is an abstraction, concerning which it is impossible to form an idea. Matter, such as we behold it, is not inert. It is infinitely active and subtile. Light, electricity, and magnetism are fluids not surpassed by thought itself in tenuity and activity: like thought they are sometimes the cause and sometimes the effect of motion; and, distinct as they are from every other class of substances with which we are acquainted, seem to possess equal claims with thought to the unmeaning distinction of immateriality.

The laws of motion and the properties of matter suffice to account for every phenome-

non, or combination of phenomena exhibited in
the Universe. That certain animals exist in
certain climates, results from the consentaneity of their frames to the circumstances of their
situation: let these circumstances be altered to
a sufficient degree, and the elements of their
composition must exist in some new combination no less resulting than the former from
those inevitable laws by which the Universe is
governed.

It is the necessary consequence of the organi-
zation of man, that his stomach should digest
his food: it inevitably results also from his
gluttonous and unnatural appetite for the flesh
of animals that his frame be diseased and his
vigor impaired; but in neither of these cases
is adaptation of means to end to be perceived.
Unnatural diet, and the habits consequent upon
its use are the means, and every complication
of frightful disease is the end, but to assort
that these means were adapted to this end by
the Creator of the world, or that human caprice
can avail to traverse the precautions of Omnipotence, is absurd. These are the consequences of the properties of organized matter.

. . . . .

What then is this harmony, this order which
you maintain to have required for its establish-
ment, what it needs not for its maintenance,
the agency of a supernatural intelligence? Inasmuch as the order visible in the Universe
requires one cause, so does the disorder whose
operation is not less clearly apparent, demand
another. Order and disorder are no more than
modifications of our own perceptions of the
relations which subsist between ourselves and
external objects, and if we are justified in inferring the operation of a benevolent power
from the advantages attendant on the former,

the evils of the latter bear equal testimony to the activity of a malignant principle, no less pertinacious in inducing evil out of good, than the other is unremitting in procuring good from evil.

If we permit our imagination to traverse the obscure regions of possibility, we may doubt-less imagine, according to the complexion of our minds, that disorder may have a relative tendency to unmingled good, or order be rela-tively replete with exquisite and subtile evil. To neither of these conclusions, which are equally presumptuous and unfounded, will it become the philosopher to assent. Order and disorder are expressions denoting our percep-tions of what is injurious or beneficial to our-selves, or to the beings in whose welfare we are compelled to sympathize by the similarity of their conformation to our own.

A beautiful antelope panting under the fangs of a tiger, a defenseless ox, groaning beneath the butcher's axe, is a spectacle which instantly awakens compassion in a virtuous and un-vitiated breast. Many there are, however, suf-ficiently hardened to the rebukes of justice and the precepts of humanity, as to regard the deliberate butchery of thousands of their species, as a theme of exultation and a source of honor, and to consider any failure in these remorseless enterprises as a defect in the sys-tem of things. The criteria of order and dis-order are as various as those beings from whose opinions and feelings they result.

Populous cities are destroyed by earthquakes, and desolated by pestilence. Ambition is every-where devoting its millions to incalculable calamity. Superstition, in a thousand shapes, is employed in brutalizing and degrading the human species, and fitting it to endure without a murmur the oppression of its innumerable tyrants. All this is abstractedly neither good nor evil, because good and evil are words employed to designate that peculiar state of our own perceptions, resulting from the encounter of any object calculated to produce pleasure or pain. Exclude the idea of relation, and the words good and evil are deprived of import.

Earthquakes are injurious to the cities which they destroy, beneficial to those whose commerce was injured by their prosperity, and indifferent to others which are too remote to be affected by their influence. Famine is good to the corn-merchant, evil to the poor, and indifferent to those whose fortunes can at all times command a superfluity. Ambition is evil to the restless bosom it inhabits, to the innumerable victims who are dragged by its ruthless thirst for infamy, to expire in every variety of anguish, to the inhabitants of the country it depopulates, and to the human race whose improvement it retards; it is indifferent with regard to the system of the Universe, and is good only to the vultures and the jackals that track the conquerors career, and to the worms who feast in security on the desolation of his progress. It is manifest that we cannot reason with respect to the universal system from that which only exists in relation to our own perceptions.

You allege some considerations in favor of a Deity from the universality of a belief in his existence.

The superstitions of the savage, and the religion of civilized Europe appear to you to conspire to prove a first cause. I maintain that it is from the evidence of revelation alone that this belief derives the slightest countenance.

That credulity should be gross in proportion to the ignorance of the mind which it enslaves, is in strict consistency with the principles of human nature. The idiot, the child, and the savage, agree in attributing their own passions and propensities to the inanimate substances by which they are either benefited or injured. The former becomes God and the latter Demons; hence prayers and sacrifices, by the means of which the rude Theologian imagines that he may confirm the benevolence of the one, or mitigate the malignity of the other. He has averted the wrath of a powerful enemy by supplications and submissions; he has secured the assistance of his neighbor by offerings; he has felt his own anger subside before the entreaties of a vanquished foe, and has cherished gratitude for the kindness of another. Therefore does he believe that the elements will listen to his vows. He is capable of love and hatred towards his fellow beings, and is variously impelled by those principles to benefit or injure them. The source of his error is sufficiently obvious. When the winds, the waves and the atmosphere, act in such a manner as to thwart or forward his designs, he attributes to them the same propensities of whose existence within himself he is conscious when he is instigated by benefits to kindness, or by injuries to revenge. The bigot of the woods can form no conception of being possessed of properties differing from his own: it requires, indeed, a mind considerably tinctured with science, and enlarged by cultivation to contemplate itself, not as the center and model of the Universe, but as one of the infinitely various multitude of beings of which it is actually composed.

There is no attribute of God which is not either borrowed from the passions and powers of the human mind, or which is not a negation. Omniscience, Omnipotence, Omnipresence, Infinity, Immutability, Incomprehensibility, and

Immateriality, are all words which designate properties and powers peculiar to organized beings, with the addition of negations, by which the idea of limitation is excluded.

That the frequency of a belief in God (for it is not universal) should be any argument in its favor, none to whom the innumerable mistakes of men are familiar, will assert. It is among men of genius and science that Atheism alone is found, but among these alone is cherished an hostility to those errors, with which the illiterate and vulgar are infected.

How small is the proportion of those who really believe in God, to the thousands who are prevented by their occupations from ever bestowing a serious thought upon the subject, and the millions who worship butterflies, bones, feathers, monkeys, calabashes and serpents. The word God, like other abstractions, signifies the agreement of certain propositions, rather than the presence of any idea. If we found our belief in the existence of God on the universal consent of mankind, we are duped by the most palpable of sophisms. The word God cannot mean at the same time an ape, a snake, a bone, a calabash, a Trinity, a Unity. Nor can that belief be accounted universal against which men of powerful intellect and spotless virtue have in every age protested.

Hume has shown, to the satisfaction of all philosophers, that the only idea which we can form of causation is derivable from the constant conjunction of objects, and the consequent inference of one from the other. We denominate that phenomenon the cause of another which we observe with the fewest exceptions to precede its occurrence. Hence it would be inadmissible to deduce the being of a God from the existence of the Universe; even if this mode of reasoning did not conduct to the monstrous conclusion of an infinity of creative and created Gods, each more eminently requiring a Creator than its predecessor.

If Power be an attribute of existing substance, substance could not have derived its origin from power. One thing cannot be at the same time the cause and the effect of another.—The word power expresses the capability of anything to be or act. The human mind never hesitates to annex the idea of power to any object of its experience. To deny that power is the attribute of being, is to deny that being can be. If power be an attribute of substance, the hypothesis of a God is a superfluous and unwarrantable assumption.

Intelligence is that attribute of the Deity, which you hold to be most apparent in the Universe. Intelligence is only known to us as a mode of animal being. We cannot conceive intelligence distinct from sensation and perception, which are attributes to organized bodies. To assert that God is intelligent, is to assert that he has ideas; and Locke has proved that ideas result from sensation. Sensation can exist only in an organized body, an organized body is necessarily limited both in extent and operation. The God of the rational Theosophies is a vast and wise animal.

You have laid it down as a maxim that the power of beginning motion is an attribute of mind as much as thought and sensation.

Mind cannot create, it can only perceive. Mind is the recipient of impressions made on the organs of sense, and without the action of external objects we should not only be deprived of all knowledge of the existence of mind, but totally incapable of the knowledge of anything. It is evident, therefore, that mind deserves to be considered as the effect, rather than the cause of motion. The ideas which suggest themselves too are prompted by the circumstances of our situation, these are the elements of thought, and from the various combinations of these our feelings, opinions, and volitions inevitably result.

That which is infinite necessarily includes that which is finite. The distinction therefore between the Universe, and that by which the Universe is upheld, is manifestly erroneous. To devise the word God, that you may express a certain portion of the universal system, can answer no good purpose in philosophy: In the language of reason, the words God and Universe are synonymous.

Thus from the principles of that reason to which you so rashly appealed to the ultimate arbiter of our dispute, have I shown that the popular arguments in favor of the being of a God are totally destitute of color. I have shown the absurdity of attributing intelligence to the cause of those effects which we perceive in the Universe, and the fallacy which lurks in the argument from design. I have shown that order is no more than a peculiar manner of contemplating the operation of necessary agents, that mind is the effect, not the cause of motion, that power is the attribute, not the origin of Being. I have proved that we can have no evidence of the existence of a God from the principles of reason.

You will have observed, from the zeal with which I have urged arguments so revolting to my genuine sentiments, and conducted to a conclusion in direct contradiction to that faith which every good man must eternally preserve, how little I am inclined to sympathize with those of my religion who have pretended to prove the existence of God by the unassisted light of reason. I confess that the necessity of a revelation has been compromised by treacherous friends to Christianity, who have maintained that the sublime, mysteries of the being of a God and the immortality of the soul are discoverable from other sources than itself.

I have proved that on the principles of that philosophy to which Epicurus, Lord Bacon, Newton, Locke, and Hume were addicted, the existence of God is a chimera.

The Christian religion then, alone, affords indisputable assurance that the world was created by the power, and is preserved by the Providence of an Almighty God, who, in justice has appointed a future life for the punishment of the vicious and the remuneration of the virtuous.

Now, O Theosophus, I call upon you to decide between Atheism and Christianity; to declare whether you will pursue your principles to the destruction of the bonds of civilized society, or wear the easy yoke of that religion which proclaims "peace upon earth, good will to all men."

THEOSOPHUS

I am not prepared at present, I confess, to reply clearly to your unexpected arguments. I assure you that no considerations, however specious, should seduce me to deny the existence of my Creator.

I am willing to promise that if, after mature deliberation, the arguments which you have advanced in favor of Atheism should appear incontrovertible, I will endeavor to adopt so much of the Christian scheme as is consistent with my persuasion of the goodness, unity and majesty of God.